Vignettes & Vinaigrettes

Vignettes & Vinaigrettes

A Memoir Of Catering
Before Food Was Hot

Carol G. Durst-Wertheim

Full Court Press
Englewood Cliffs, New Jersey

Published in the United States of America
by Full Court Press, 601 Palisade Avenue,
Englewood Cliffs, NJ 07632
fullcourtpress.com

ISBN 978-1-946989-50-5
Library of Congress Control Number: 2020905404

Editing and book design by Barry Sheinkopf

Cover art by GG Kopilak

Author photo by Kevan Full

Dedication

To my catering crews: Michael Hoelscher, Max McGuire, Lilia Chelala, Thom Smyth, Bobby Betke, John Whitney, Millie Tirelli, Radhica Ramsamy, Anita Farber, Jim Kennedy, Aurora Cahinhininan, and so many others, who carried New American Catering Corporation on their shoulders.

To Les Wertheim, my husband, who continues to support my next chapters and to our beloved son, Will, a most interesting fellow.

To Hy and Flo Goldsmith, who marveled at every step; to sisters Joan Goldsmith Gurfield and Nancy Rita Wolfe, and their families, who never ceased to cheer.

Acknowledgements

I am deeply grateful to Dr. Abigail Burnham Bloom, for encouraging me to write and keep on writing, for many years of the kindest friendship, and for the group of one hundred words.

Dr. Doris Friedensohn, who helped complete my Kirkland education, fifty years after we left the Hill, we came full circle as friends. She introduced me to Barry Sheinkopf, who held my feet to the fire and talked food and editorial fine points with grace, ease, and the confidence to lift any soufflé.

Dr. Marion Nestle, for her extraordinary trust and attention to an adjunct's query, bringing me forward into the twenty-first century. Full stop.

Dr. Roni Natov, who guided my early efforts to write about this work and steered me safely through doctoral studies at the Union Institute and University.

I thank the many writing teachers, colleagues and friends who moved me through college, graduate school, a doctoral program, to the burbs and into print. Among the best: Lianne Birkhold, Katherine Hagstrum, Bob Keefer, Kate Austin, Annie Hauck-Lawson, Tisha Bender, Andrea Black Jeffries, Beverly Tobin, Mindy Lewis, Madge McKeithen, AnnaLee Wilson, Trish Lobenfeld, Ellen Fried, Adele Kaplan, Charlene Newburg, Mimi Krohn, Felice Schwartz, Katherine Tobin, Becca Marin, Carol Moore, Yvonne von Pesch, Marcela Lococo Bahillo, Jon Zimmerman, Ilene Cummings, Anita Lands Glasgall, Helene Bass-Wichelhaus, Libby Antarsh, Bonnie Lee Black, Terry Solowey.

I learned so much from my culinary teachers, food industry mentors and inspirations: Jack Ubaldi, Nick Malgieri, Michael Bradshaw, Robert Posch, Melissa Lord, Susan Anderson, Pat Bartholomew, Leslie Revsin, Pat Baird, Joyce Goldstein, Elizabeth Crossman, Irene Sax, Meryl Evans, Cara De Silva, Anne Mendelsohn, Betty Fussell, Bill Liederman and John "Q." Lowy, Hilary Baum, Frances Lappe, Jane Umanoff and Beau Parsons, Judy Arnold, Sarabeth Levine, Ariane Daguin, Joan Gussow, Julia Delle Croce, Lou, Sal, and Marie Di Palo of Di Palo's Fine Foods, Lisa Ekus, Renee Marton, Jonathan Deutsch, Sara Moulton, Barbara Sibley, Suzanne Fass, Miriam Rubin, Nancy Jessup, Sabrina Buck Scher, and many other members of the New York Women's Culinary Alliance.

I had the good fortune to work with many stunning students at New York University, Food Studies who have carved their own unique paths. Among them: Lisa DeLange, Agatha Krishchenko, Tomoko Iwaki, Yuri Asaro, Erica Lesser, Orasri Liangthanasarn, Surbhi Sahni, Jennifer O'Flanagan, Robynne Maii, Kendra Lott, Lucy Norris, Krystal Ford, Gypsy Lovett, Linda Berzok, in addition to students taking thirty-plus years of classes with me in culinary schools, colleges, and universities.

This book cover is the art of GG Kopilak, who drew me into the Pleasantville Garden Club.

I thank Carlos Guajardo, for keeping our house in suburbia standing, and Martha and Eduardo Ramon, who have kept that house and garden in order. One night, they drove across the Tappan Zee Bridge (now the Mario Cuomo Bridge) to a rural location in Rockland County to help cater a private school parents' association event. As the evening moved from start-up chaos to more orderly dessert service, they looked over at me and quietly laughed together. I pressed for a translation until they shared: "She works like an immigrant." I never received a higher compliment.

Table of Contents

———

INTRODUCTION

S EX, DRUGS, FIRE—THAT'S ALL FINE and great media drama, but those stories have little to do with my years in the food industry, and those are not the dreams and goals I've heard from people who aspired to culinary careers over the last forty years.

Set in New York City in 1980–2000, *Vignettes & Vinaigrettes* reflects the second wave of the Women's Movement, as women entered, returned, and remained in the labor market in unprecedented numbers at the end of the twentieth century. Commercial cooking, perceived as a vocational option for those not academically gifted in earlier times, or as employment for an underclass of ethnic and minority women, took on a different significance during these years, when some highly educated and creative women, of diverse backgrounds, pushed their way into industry. Some food work assumed a new status, and the range of employment and business options expanded. Some women received significant compensation for their creative work and their customized services, but ambivalent attitudes toward, and assumptions about, food workers lingered. Looking back to the end of the twentieth century, before everything moved at internet speeds, there were not many women who made Martha Stewart's money, held Ruth Reichl's glamorous jobs, or were paid for Mimi Sheraton's sleuthing. We were not all drug-and-alcohol-abusing waitress/actresses, Italian grandmothers, or perky TV pop-stars either. Women on the TV *Food Network* too often were slathered in buttercream, slashing at some hostile stove, or made into caricatures staring seductively at a camera up close as we, the voyeurs, witnessed total meltdown.

However, women wrote more guidebooks, textbooks, and cookbooks than most mortals will ever cook their way through; many women edited cookbooks, tested recipes, and marketed a range of goods and services long before the internet made everyone a culinary genius. (BTW: Who wrote the content commercializing all the websites?)

Classes in food studies and nutrition burgeoned, and local/sustainable food system issues came to the fore then, now part of daily conversations: Many leaders of the current food "movement" are women. But the recent history of women in the food industries, with their many nuanced stories, has been omitted from most of the media attention. *It is long past time to hear the stories of the invisible entrepreneurs of that generation, women working in the smaller food industry businesses, in all those undefined and uncounted, but professional, roles outside restaurant kitchens.*

In just a few decades Americans moved from the ideal of the June Cleaver Mom (do you remember 1957–63 *Leave it to Beaver* on TV?) baking cookies at home, wearing pearls and high heels as she vacuumed her suburban living room, to a twenty-first century reality of families consuming more than half their meals away from home and using "prepared and semi-prepared foods" for many of their at-home meals and family events. Today, prepared food bars are ubiquitous at supermarkets, deli, and specialty shops (who prepares all that food?), and new permutations of home-meal delivery continue to emerge in urban centers throughout this country.

Women returned to the labor market at the end of the twentieth century in huge numbers, and someone other than "mom" began to provide those "home meal replacements." Some of the people preparing dinner were domestic workers: immigrant and minority women, hired as caregivers in affluent homes to provide assistance on the "second shift," where Arlie Hochschild identified the issues of working moms who needed help (since domestic partners did not necessarily pick up the slack) to keep their homes functioning. Sometimes, food was prepared by seasoned professionals, running large and small businesses, offering services as private chefs or for catered events, business entertaining, large-scale parties, and family dinners. Some of these professional culinary workers set up spectacular events, created new products, promoted food trends, addressed issues of nutrition, defined organic foods, developed the personal chef services and the partially prepared meals we now take for granted. *However, we do not have a realistic count of the numbers of women in these various roles, or much idea of what the work was like then or now: This work was not described then and is still not fully accounted for by the U.S. Department of Labor Bureau of Labor Statistics.*

Although the food industry appears to be male-dominated, in truth more women than men actually hold the jobs (predominantly the part-time, low-level, poorly paid positions). The National Restaurant Association claims that fifty-three percent of this nation's food workers are women (the Women's Foodservice Forum claims it's fifty-seven percent); however, these numbers reflect the lowest ranks among food workers, which is not the work culinary students aspire to find or the businesses they hope to create. These numbers decline sharply as you look further up the ranks for women chefs, managers, COOs, CEOs, and corporate board positions. Women still chef fewer than seven percent of independent restaurants.

Men's published stories don't reveal much about the small, start-up businesses that proliferated at the end of the twentieth century. Media attention focuses on outrageous stories, most about men, but I am tired of the reruns of Anthony Bourdain eating worms, Guy Fieri grossly overfeeding himself, or Bobby Flay battling fictitious culinary arts competitions: food porn. Ed and Tom Lee's *Hotbox* is tracking some catering businesses, but their stories don't cover the whole industry. The "how-to" books don't come close to touching the reality of this work. Missing from the men's accounts of their food work is a range of personal encounters that color so much of women's work, especially catering, and communications around food trends, health concerns, and farm sustainability.

The desire to work closely with food, and the impulse to connect and to bond with clients and staff, expresses a perspective different from that of *Food Network* commercials, competitive and dramatic cooking-as-performance-art, or large scale, massive feeding operations. The emotional contact with food is often the principal reason students give for choosing the industry. But is that motivation too "quiet" for TV entertainment? Is it too close to the family nurturing provided by women, unpaid for centuries, that is missing from so many lives today? Is that emotional connection somehow devalued as "female"? It was precisely that emotional component I witnessed in my years of teaching in culinary arts programs, and I have often asked, "Do women define their work and their success differently from men who cook professionally? Why are their business ventures less able to attract publicity and capital investment?" Asking these academic questions reveals that very little is actually known about women entrepreneurs in the food industry from sociological, statistical, and anecdotal perspectives. *The social forces of the late twentieth century created opportunities in the food industry for entrepreneurial women, but the stories of their work have not received the same attention as the dramatic episodes staged by men, and their numbers are not accurately available—anywhere!*

It is striking to note some of the recent shift in our society's food concerns: Now a huge demand exists for both global and local products, and organic and specialty ingredients, which has triggered sizeable industry shifts. Now increasing public concern has arisen about the eating habits of our children, and a growing population is learning to cook from TV and internet sources. The end of the twentieth century saw many women driving and fulfilling those changing trends, but their stories are largely unknown.

Less of a divide separates home cooks from professional ones these days as well: Access to professional-grade equipment and 24/7 internet instructions empower interested home cooks to try dishes they would not have attempted thirty years ago, when instructions were available only in the odd copy of *Gourmet* magazine. Home cooks learned from Julia Child, James Beard, Irma Rombach, Fannie Farmer or *The Settlement Cookbook*, while professional training reflected Escoffier's rules and some rather ponderous textbooks. *It is too narrow to define culinary professionals as only restaurant chefs. More women than men train in culinary schools these days, and more move into a range of professional roles, which are still not accurately counted in government labor statistics. Therefore, we still don't know who these women really are, or how many are trying to create businesses. We are unsure who succeeds in culinary work, how they train and build careers, or how they will create work–life balances through their years. Undercounting leads to underrepresentation and, unfortunately, devaluation of women's contributions.*

My work reflects that earlier social change: how women returning to the labor market at the end of the twentieth century affected the ways we ate, cooked or did not cook, and learned about food and cooking—all of which is so very different today, influenced in part by the internet. I believe we need to record the creativity of the individuals working at the end of the twentieth century, before that time of transition is forgotten: No, this is *not* the first time cooks have invented potato salad! There is a lot of history about women's work that is still missing from the canon, not taught even in culinary schools. These stories, about individuals and small business, allow the reader to stand at my elbow, at the intersection of gender, race, and class roles, nurturing with food and professional food service work in the time just before working with food became "hot."

My stories, written as I looked up from my pots and pans, my cutting board, and the back stairwell, offer portraits and encounters I experienced, experiences shared by others in this industry, entrepreneurs and artists, those who worked beside me, and people I met along the way. I share my personal connections with crews, clients, family and the foods we served. The arc of these stories moves from my entry into a burgeoning 1980s culinary world through relocation to the suburbs and a lingering sense of dislocation, a span of thirty-five-plus years.

Like the dressing that coats and binds, my title refers to the sweet and savory emulsions, bonding salads and side dishes, yet allowing all ingredients to be seen, balancing the portraits we should have of all those who worked, and continue to work, in this complex industry.

Early Years

1979–81

Why Bill Hired Me

THE SHORT ANSWER: I HAD CREDENTIALS, smarts, could get along with anyone, and was not overly impressed with myself. Also, it was apparent that I thought independently and could live outside the box, not needing job structure or a lock-step career path. I had no issue challenging the usual and customary way things were done, but I was polite about it. I spoke well and could stand before the New School administrators swapping academic lingo, lead a tour through the kitchens and recruit students by the dozen, swing by the students changing in the locker room, and not freak out at the language, drugs, nudity, and knives flashing by. Hey, I was twenty-seven and could carry myself on four-inch stilettos.

The longer answer weaves back through my life history, but I don't have to bore you with all the details. Suffice it to say, I had a "spotty" undergraduate history, complete with a Me Too moment that changed my arts career trajectory. I focused in graduate school on women's career planning, bounced through jobs in academia, then landed as a research associate at Catalyst, a not-for-profit organization dedicated to women's career development. There, working under a prestigious FIPSE (Fund for the Improvement of Post-Secondary Education) grant, I met Adele Kaplan, part of the team representing Rutgers University. We knew one another through a professional association (NAW-DAC, the National Association of Women Deans, Administrators and Counselors), and she introduced me to her son.

Can you believe he listened to his mother? That's how I came to be interviewed for the position as director of the restaurant school Bill Liederman was creating, though I knew nothing about the restaurant industry. After Catalyst, I had moved to New York State Department of Labor to coordinate the Displaced Homemakers Program until a budget crisis forced me out of my office on the seventy-third floor of the World Trade Center. By my late twenties I had some chops in academic, not-for-profit, and government circles. I had academic credentials, writing and verbal presentation skills, and I understood how to put a legitimate academic curriculum in front of the New School dean. Bill needed the dean's support and approval to proceed with his extraordinary idea of organizing the New York Restaurant School as a full-time eighteen-week, twelve-credit program. With my resume attached, Bill's proposal flew past the Department of Education, Adult Education Division, in Albany, under the aegis of the New School's licensure. There were no issues with government regulations, and we began to recruit a first class for January, 1981.

My NAWDAC dinner group gathered at my apartment the

night before I was going to begin working with Bill and John Lowy in December 1980, and everyone toasted Adele for connecting me with her son's new venture.

Just after they left, I heard sirens and saw flashing ambulance lights heading down Broadway. I turned on the news and watched Yoko Ono struggle to break free from the press at St. Luke's Emergency Room. Weeping as I cleaned up, I heard shrieking from the streets; John Lennon had been shot three blocks from my apartment.

I dragged myself to my new work the next day; all any of us could do was sit around and cry. But the day after that, I began to interview faculty and to scratch out the first tentative schedules. We were all deeply saddened to lose John Lennon, but we had a new opportunity on the table, and the clock was ticking, so we launched our new culinary venture.

My Culinary Education Begins

T O HELP ME UNDERSTAND what culinary education was about, Bill Liederman (the kid brother of David Lieder-man of David's Cookies—it's a small world), asked me to watch a few classes in the Saucier Cuisine test kitchen on the corner of Madison Avenue and Thirty-fourth Street. This was the space where David was developing a demi-glace sauce base. He already had David's Cookies and a restaurant on the Upper East Side, but I didn't know much about that. I wasn't sure I would find much to respect there. In the Department of Labor, the food industry had a terrible reputation for abusing workers.

At the time we first met, in late 1979, I was traveling all over New York State: hauling into Buffalo in February, arriving in Canton up in the North Country on a twelve-seater prop plane, cashing State vouchers for buses and trains everywhere else as Coordinator of the Displaced Homemaker Program for the New York State Department of Labor.

Bill took a table to promote his cooking school at a conference I organized in Brooklyn, in June 1980, for seven hundred women and dozens of not-for-profit agencies, employers, and politicians willing to focus on the issues of older women. I was busy and didn't have much interest in what Bill was saying about food industry opportunities; I didn't see what the big deal was about cooking classes. But we kept talking over the summer.

Bill tried to explain what a "vocational" class would look like, and what an "avocational" class meant. He had cobbled together a six-week "professional" program taught in the Saucier kitchen and he was now trying to expand that into a full-time eighteen-week program for the New School for Social Research. Gradually, I learned he wanted me as director. He and John Lowy, his partner and sidekick for years of adventures, would run the avocational classes, building an ever-increasing assortment of classes designed for home cooks, while I was to build this professional program. At least, that was how it was originally planned. We had no idea the professional program would catapult us onto a burgeoning New York City food scene, set the pattern for dozens of other culinary schools throughout the nation, and provide a major route for career changers and people who wanted to enter the food industry without spending years at the Culinary Institute of America up in Hyde Park on the Hudson River.

By the fall of 1980, we were talking more seriously, and Bill suggested I watch Pat Bartholomew, Nick Malgieri, and Jack Ubaldi to see a sampling of the classes he was describing. His plan was to keep these classes going in their present Saucier test-kitchen space until the new facility, with three commercial teaching kitchens and a fourth kitchen connected to a restaurant space, was constructed—oh, in a month or so, certainly by the end of January 1981, he estimated. Bill and John walked me through the construction site at 27 West Thirty-fourth Street and conducted my first official interview there as I wobbled around on a tipsy, torn old office chair, John sat on an up-turned milk crate, and Bill balanced himself on a rickety cane-baked chair with a hole punched through the seat. They wanted to be sure I wasn't too proper to handle work on a messy, unfinished project. I was coming down, literally, from the Seventy-third floor of the World Trade Tower II, harbor view, and they were offering me an office, with no windows, the size of my conference table. They wanted to be perfectly clear this was the deal: hard work creating an adult-training program from scratch, while workers finished the construction. Nothing would be fancy, just the very best ingredients. Would I give up my prestigious government job working for the New York State Commissioner of Labor? Turned out, I had to, but that wasn't clear yet.

Pat's was the first class they scheduled for me. This was fall 1980: I watched as Pat Bartholomew scraped Gruyere cheese into her Romaine salad. She carefully explained how to handle, wash, and keep lettuce fresh and crisp. She spoke about extra-virgin olive oil (in 1980, I didn't know what that *was*), freshly grated peppercorns, sea salt, and sherry vinegar, in balance to create vinaigrette. I had never tasted a salad like that. I had not thought of contrasts and textures in my salads, had not really noticed whether my croutons were freshly toasted and crispy. I had mostly been eating the rancid ones Pepperidge Farms put in boxes and left too long on grocers' shelves.

But this woman didn't fit my preconception and stereotype of a brute cook slamming pots and cursing at staff. She was tall and elegant, erudite and educated. She worked in a corporate dining room by day, taught and was taking a graduate degree by night. Well, that wasn't what I had expected for the evening. Neither was the salad. I thought I should look further into this cooking business.

Nick Malgieri's class met a few days later, in the late afternoon as I recall. It was dark gray outside, late fall in New York City, hovering between rain and sleet, pending snow. Nick was introducing a group of well-heeled ladies to "Spectacular Holiday Baking." He had also come out of the Trade Towers: He had been an opening pastry chef at Windows on the World. When I first met him, he was a slender, small man with a rapier wit, capacity for a multitude of languages, and the engaging flamboyance I later came to recognize as his trademark performance style.

He was demonstrating *Bouche de Noel* with the deep mastery that mesmerized all his students. His verbal repartee was sophisticated: He noted clues to watch as the eggs were beaten while he teased a woman with long nails painted to perfection. His strong, quick hands rolled the chocolate genoise around the fabulous buttercream, set the log and a smaller branch at a jaunty angle, draped it all with smooth, silky dark chocolate ganache, and then began decorating with tiny meringue mushrooms he'd dusted in cocoa powder (Dutch process no less), all the while calmly explaining the history of this traditional treat. Of course, it was *fabulous!*

Over the years I watched him grow from a skinny guy dancing at the clubs all night, flinging exquisite pastry all day, into a masterful TV presence, a traveling road show promoting his many baking books with great wit and intellectual presence. He has a remarkable palate, a refined sophistication. He is a consummate performer. Nick got me in the sweet tooth. Once he showed me *Bouche de Noel*, everything else looked easy.

My third class, the following morning, was butchering instruction with Jack Ubaldi. His warm eyes seduced me in moments. That gentleman, retired from a lifetime of heavy work in butchering and restaurant cooking, loved the idea of a "lady boss" not quite half his age. It was obvious we were friends from his first hello.

"Ciao, Bella!" Notes from a resonant tenor, he offered a loving embrace; eyes lit by his own smile, he was generosity personified. Jack demonstrated butchering while he cooked. He spoke of life, of *his* life. He sang, soothed students, and enjoyed himself as he demonstrated his skills. He eased his knives along the muscles of meat, respectful, accurate as a surgeon, accurate with an artist's eye.

He would weave in a story about his restaurant in the bootleg days. He was there again cooking, with people partying around him all night long. Then he would find his way to the Gansevoort Meat Market the next morning to buy meat for the following night. Jack was always working, in love with feeding people. The long hours meant nothing: Where else would he be? His life was the restaurant; the restaurant was his life. Later on, it was the same with his butcher shop.

"Did I ever tell you about Ed Koch buying the Newport steaks? It was this triangular muscle I used to cut into a nice steak—a good price and it was very popular. People wanted it! They asked me what it was called. I went home and watched on TV—there was an advertisement for these cigarettes, Newports? And they showed a sailboat, and the sail was just the shape of these steaks, so I named them Newport steaks! Just like that! I sold a lot of them. People really liked them! Well, Ed Koch used to live in the neighborhood, before he was mayor you know, and he'd stop in to buy them. He was a very nice man, and a good customer!"

By the time I met him, Jack had already sold the Florence Meat Market on Jones Street to his assistant, Tony, but he couldn't stand being retired, out of touch with people, so he went over to the New School and asked if they wanted him to teach some cooking or butchering classes in their cafeteria. Thus, the New School got into the culinary education business. Then Bill inherited Jack as they began to expand programs.

Bill wanted me to set up a legitimate curriculum, to show the New School he had a *bona fide* educator running the eighteen-week program, and I took the job, creating the New York Restaurant School. We worked incredible hours on curriculum and scheduling. We found teachers, recruited students and found them jobs. We worked out systems of operations, protocols, we opened the restaurant with the earliest trial versions of POS (point-of-sale) computer systems, we negotiated the squabbles and struggles of creating a thriving school that opened doors for people who wanted to enter the food industry.

Then, Jack made lunch. No measuring cups in sight, Jack would cook the meat his class had just butchered and he would make sauce for pasta. A salad appeared, lightly dressed with a simple vinaigrette, loaves of crusty bread, a few bottles of wine. We had our very own Strega Nona: There was always enough food for whoever wanted to eat. He just knew how to cook for us all, as an experienced traveler (or lover) knows the terrain, and I began to understand culinary education.

I Fed Al Pacino

NO, I WON'T TELL YOU WHAT HE ATE. I promised I wouldn't. Everyone wants to know what it was like, feeding him, so I'll tell you what I can without breaking my promise not to violate his privacy.

He was acting in *American Buffalo* on Broadway, living in his own home in New York City, but he could not just go around the corner, pop into the diner, and order food. Sunglasses and a fedora pulled low were not enough to camouflage his distinctive face. What a tremendous energy drain to be such a recognized face when everyone feels entitled to sidle up and start a conversation! How could he concentrate the enormous energy needed for a live performance of raging fury at every show if he was interrupted for a signature at any bite?

The job as his private chef came to me in a unique way. I had been the Director of the New York Restaurant School, a position of some authority, which included a particularly energy-draining requirement to pay attention to everyone with a question. I had students, culinary and management faculty, other administrators, guests dining in the restaurant on Thirty-fourth Street, delivery people, lost tourists—all popping their personal questions the moment they saw me. The job also demanded tact, an ability to keep my mouth shut at times, and a capacity to work independently, without a lot of strokes. These might seem like contradictory qualifications, but they overlapped most days.

Once I left the job as Director, I enrolled in the program (yeah, I know it sounds odd, but it's true), learned to cook professionally, and planned to start my own catering business. The man who took over one of my responsibilities, for Placement Services, received a job order from "Mary." She was a friend of one of our cooking school graduates who was already involved in a new restaurant venture. He suggested that Mary call the school and see if they could send over someone who could be "discreet" and cook for a famous person. Discretion seemed the primary qualification, so the placement officer thought of me. I was given Mary's telephone number, but no one knew who the famous person was or exactly what would be needed. But the school administrators knew I could handle "discretion." They hoped that, by the time I completed the course, I'd be able to cook. I hoped parties or events might develop from private cooking into some catering.

When I called, Mary gave me a few details: the address where the meals were to be served, and what the schedule might look like. I would need to be flexible. She asked if I would be willing to "audition," to cook a few meals.

I said, "Yes, sure. Will we start with a meal for one, or will there be guests? Do I need to bring my own pots? Will someone let me in, say an hour before dinner is needed?" Reasonable questions, I thought. She laughed and said she had to get back to me. When she did, she suggested some favorite foods, told me to bring pots since no one seemed to know what was in the cupboards, and we chose a date for my audition.

"And may I ask, for whom shall I be cooking?"

Somehow that question had not been asked or answered during the first call. She giggled; we could communicate so easily already. "Al Pacino. I'll let you in Thursday," she said.

Wow, I thought. I really admired this astounding actor and thought it would be a great gig to describe to my grandchildren. I had none, not even a child, at that point, but I was optimistic. This tale has proven to be enduring: Any time I am asked who I have cooked for, if I mention Al Pacino among a list of clients, he is the one people always pick up on.

I think a person has a right to privacy, even as a mega-star, but some people believe a loss of privacy comes with that territory. Some newspapers pay handsomely for tidbits of personal information, gossip, intimate details, so paparazzi harass the famous, right into tunnels of death, for a flash of the personal.

I will share two memorable encounters, but not what he ate:

I screwed up my courage once to ask him about his work. "May I ask why you took that role in *Scarface*?"

He looked at me, then over at Mary, who was present that day for other matters. She smiled gently at him, and he looked back at me. Very patiently, he explained, "I had a chance to work with Brian De Palma." I should have understood what that meant to him professionally, but I didn't at the time, and I naively went on, "But why, with all that violence?"

He had nothing further to say, and I could not draw him out for another syllable. I'm lucky he didn't fire me for the implied criticism, but he was fielding so much worse during the early controversy in response to the film. I didn't know it would grow into a classic of the 1980s. Watching the film now, it appears to me as a brilliant portrayal of "the lion within the man," as Pacino later described the role himself—and the film sure seems less violent by today's standards.

One evening, later in the spring, I let myself into the apartment to find a meeting taking place in the living room.

"Would you like me to come back later?"

Al looked up and said, "It's okay, go ahead with what you're doing."

I understood it was a business meeting, but I didn't listen for details as I finished cooking in the kitchen, across a counter pass-through. I was absorbed in my preparation, watching my timing to bring several elements together at the same point, trying to finish with finesse.

Just as I began setting up his dinner plate, Al called to me, "Carol, we're two for dinner tonight."

"I'll be set up in just a minute." I'd had no advance warning, but I had purchased a rather large portion that day, which I divided into two smaller servings. I revised my presentation and set two plates. "Dinner is ready. Good night, gentlemen."

I was on my way down in the elevator before I recognized

the adrenalin rush. I reached the street and let out my breath, a sigh and a tremendous, loud laugh. I had survived a major improv before the eyes of a masterful actor, and no one knew what I had pulled off until I told Mary about it the next day. We could share a laugh by then, my lucky menu choice, but she was quick to apologize on Al's behalf, and it never did happen again.

When the show closed months later, Al went out to the West Coast for a few months. When he came back east, he spent some time at his home upstate, some time in the city. Whenever she had a chance, Mary called me, told me which home and about how many to expect for dinner. I put Sunday dinners on the table at his country home after he had finished basketball and rough-housing with friends. I heard a high-energy crowd happy to share a comforting dinner. I was happy to serve those dinners: steaming, fragrant, fresh. I worked in this way over two years and grew to appreciate how many people were needed behind the scenes to sustain famous lives. I learned how many of those people were not trustworthy: things were stolen, tales were told, lies were sold. I understood how Pacino had to distance himself from many of the people he needed to rely on to make his household function, as they served in intimate capacities, to handle everything.

When he took a role in a film that brought him back to the West Coast for most of a year, Mary let me know and we said respectful and kindly goodbyes. It's been over thirty years since I last cooked for him, and I know there are people who would pay me today for information about Al Pacino, but I still won't tell you what he ate.

Starting Up
A Service Business

1981–83

Nursing Excellence

THE NURSING ADMINISTRATORS FOUGHT hard for a budget, a date, space, and a keynote speaker to honor members of the staff. One administrator, Joan, was a friend, and thought of me to help with her New York event; another administrator, Angie became a friend very quickly.

The hospital food service could only conceive of a menu and staffing that blew way past anything like the nurses' budget. Clearly, they were not interested in servicing the event, so they gave me permission to cater it on their property. Hundreds of the hospital nurses were invited and encouraged to bring friends and families to watch as a few of them stood before the gathering and, recognized by the hospital leadership, receive plaques for their tenure at the hospital and their extraordinary service.

I had to provide a really, *really* low-budget menu, but I wanted to help Joan create a successful event, a gesture to counter the tense climate of union struggles in hospitals in the mid-1980s. The menu would be vegetarian, to accommodate the diverse ethnic makeup and dietary restrictions typical of a large urban hospital, so Mother Nature did most of the prep work.

I gathered a respectful, cheerful crew and rented a fifteen-foot U-Haul to cart everything over to the hospital. I intended to set up a spectacular display: mountains of perfect fruits with cascades of delectable nuts and dried fruits tumbling over baskets set at eye level on top of draped boxes, colorfully clothed buffet tables, dips and chips and crudités in great variety, and sparkling, clear beverages at the bars.

I wanted to help the hospital thank these working people despite the political tensions running beneath the surface. The event was as important to the nurses as any confirmation, graduation, or name day might have been: a public honoring of great significance among those rarely acknowledged for their services.

I had several catering adventures getting this event started.

As we were pulling some dollies out to the truck, my Aussie bartender yelped. He had thrown out his back, was out of commission, and could barely stand up. "We're on our way to the hospital, guys," I said to the others who gathered around. "Carry him into the truck, keep him flat on the floor, and please put your suit bags around and under him. Make him comfortable as you can. I'll try not to hit any bumps." It seemed the self-evident solution to me; I would worry about worker's compensation and his immigration status later.

Then a crudité basket containing about twenty pounds of cut veggies tumbled off a dolly and into the gutter. "Leave it," I sighed. "Just bring the basket. We'll make do with the others."

I wasn't going to feed anyone street-spilt veggies the pigeons were already gathering around.

The staff tried to scoop together the pieces that hadn't hit the ground, saving me something, trying to pull with me, but we had to let that go.

I had to rely on ice delivered by Amado, the uptown service, because my usual company, Diamond Ice, would not cross the line into Amado's territory. "Territory? Since when?" I had asked.

"Remember the arrangements with the dumpster guys, Carol?" my iceman had asked. Just a few months earlier several restaurants had broken plate glass windows, defining the terms of business and ensuring that guaranteed territories remained guaranteed. He wished me luck and said, "Call me when you're working downtown again."

I drove the truck gingerly to Mt. Sinai Hospital, stopped at the Emergency entrance to drop off my injured Aussie, then turned into a courtyard where we were allowed to unload, but not to park, according to hospital security guards.

I was needed to direct the set-up; who else had a license on them to drive this thing? "I do," said Max. "There are meters on Madison, and we can park legally after 7:00."

It was 4:00. I couldn't lose Max for three hours! "What about the garages?" I asked him. "See if the one on Ninety-ninth, or the one up on 104th, will take this thing. Offer them a few bucks." I pressed cash into Max's palm and wished him luck. If he could not get legally parked in forty-five minutes, I told him to come back and I would fight the hospital courtyard security detail to allow us to leave the van in a corner, just for the duration of the party, as the administration had initially promised. That might happen too—for more cash.

I had set aside enough time for set-up, but I was down two staff. I was glad that Tristate Party Rentals had delivered everything they were supposed to; those items had been secured near the lobby in advance of the party. More cash showed my appreciation to *that* security team for receiving it and not allowing the hospital staff to "mistakenly" appropriate items before we arrived. The rental order was just tables, cloths, and chairs, but buffet tables are useful around hospitals, someone might have liked a new tablecloth for a large table at home, ailing patients were always looking for extra chairs in that lobby, and caterers pay if rental returns don't match the shipment orders.

I moved into a corner where some screens defined my "kitchen" space, and I shared my floor plan as the staff discreetly changed into tuxedos and moved to open up the rented buffet tables and unwrap tablecloths.

The lobby quickly became our stage. Tables went under available lighting. Traffic flows were considered and angles adjusted as assiduously as bowties. Two bars would offer white wine and sodas only. I would not serve red wine over the marble floor no matter how well polished it was or how careful everyone tried to be: Such stains really turned people against caterers.

I was rearranging the crudité baskets, filling in the gap from the earlier mishap, when Max appeared, just twenty minutes later! He had found a spot on a side street. "Keep the cash for good luck!" I exclaimed, hoping we wouldn't find the tires slashed when we went to retrieve the vehicle in a few hours.

As we were setting up for the event following the ceremony in the auditorium, people strolled toward it through the lobby. Those nurses to be singled out for awards came with corsages pinned to their shoulders or wrists, dressed in their Sunday best, some in colorful saris, some wearing Easter hats, bouffant and intricate hairdos, heels and feathered finery. Sometimes it was their mothers who wore the corsages and beamed with pride at daughters who worked so hard and served for so many years. Many kids came too, enjoying the break from the usual after-school routines. The boys were happy to have a big space to roam, fighting the constriction of their suits and ties, eager to slide across the buffed lobby floors, swipe something off a table, and scoot off in another direction. The girls wore their flouncy dresses, bows in their braids, and were much more restrained. Husbands came too, awkwardly decked out in ill-fitting, rarely worn suits, but most wore gleaming smiles.

We had the cartons upended on top of the buffet tables, draped them with extra tablecloths and we were just beginning to load large, spectacular apples, pears, and perfect oranges into the baskets, creating a fruit mountain, when the two nursing administrators came out into the lobby from the auditorium to give us a ten-minute warning. Their keynote speaker, scheduled to speak for forty-five minutes, was finishing a bit early, after about twelve.

My eyes said it all. They both put their pocketbooks down behind my screen and began helping us heave to. The bartenders doubled their pace, rapidly cracking open soda bottles and taking corks halfway out of the wine. Anticipating the rush, the bartenders enabled people to help themselves without explosions that could damage dresses.

Everyone else was tossing the beautiful fruits out of their wrappers and onto the tables just as fast as their hands could go. I tore open the bags of nuts and tossed them wherever they landed. No order was possible: we simply had to get the food onto the table before 350 people came pouring out of the auditorium. They would not pause long at the bar, and there would be no chance to get close enough to replenish these tables.

I kicked empty cartons under the buffets just as the waves broke out of containment; I could hear applause, whistles, and thunderous footsteps. I retreated to the "kitchen" as the staff dragged partial bags and boxes under the draped tables and back into my corner. They shoved what they could behind the screens for me to stack and sort and then plowed out bravely into the tide, carrying small black bussing trays, attempting to clear and pick up before things spilled and were ground underfoot into that marble floor.

In about fifteen minutes, it was all over. Many of the nurses were scheduled back on duty upstairs, so they loaded up napkins, piled fruits into the uplifted hems of their sweaters, and stuffed their uniform pockets, grabbed liters of soda off the bars, and left. In practically no time, the 350 were reduced to fifty; Joan and Angie fell into chairs, a bit shocked at the *tsunami*. My cool, experienced staff condensed inventory, repaired the arrangements, opened more wine, picked up as much of the mess as they could, offered some courtesy to older guests moving more slowly, and found some humor in the way the event had run.

"Did you see the way they snatched everything so fast?"

"Wow, faster than I could open the bottles, they were taken —before I could pour!"

"The kids were amazing—they were stuffing the fruit into their jacket pockets. Wait until their moms see how stretched that new suit is!"

"What? Didn't you see the moms stuffing their pocket-books?"

We had been booked for a two-hour party, but only a few nurses came down off their shifts to see what foods might be left during that second hour. Most of the guests cleared out with their stash within half an hour of the speeches. The party seemed more a free-food frenzy than the mellow cocktails the nursing administrators had pictured. The nurses' families were taking home groceries, treats they did not usually buy for themselves. The honoring was not experienced in quite the intended way, but it was memorable. Everyone dove in with such gusto! There were no polite manners there, no cocktail party behavior. Neither was there any food left over for me to wrap up and worry over; no food was wasted that night. Even the dips were transferred into plastic bar cups—most people left my glass bowls behind when I asked them to—and taken upstairs to share with colleagues still on duty during the celebration. They took all the food and shared it: The event was a community festival, although that may not have been the intention.

We were able to shut down and clean up within the two

hours. It was fast, loud, and joyful, not too long on polite conversation, but intense in its message. The hospital clearly needed to recognize and appreciate their nurses, and apparently they needed to increase their wages as well, which did happen in the next decades through multiple rounds of union negotiations. Nurses deserved respect and a living wage: I just happened to see the beginning of that wave, as nursing staff all over the country began the fight to gain proper valuation for their care and service. There were very few male nurses back then; only with medic training in military service, and when the salaries and benefits increased after union threats and negotiations, did the profession attract men.

After the party, we were happy when Max brought up the van unharmed; it had survived its time on the street in Spanish Harlem. My injured Australian was released from the hospital, on bed rest for a few days but set to work gigs the following week.

I was hired to cater many events by the Mt. Sinai nursing administrators for years afterward. I would bring my most life-loving staff along to create parties in Central Park for the Transplantation Department, where Angie led an extraordinary team of caregivers, and their lead surgeon understood how important it was to celebrate the lives he extended and cheer on those who cared for his patients.

THE FIRST YEAR ANGIE CALLED, just after the Nursing Excellence event, she was apologetic. "Carol, we're really not sure how many people will come, but we'd like to have a big picnic in the park." Angie—a big, bold powerhouse—had fought the budget fight for the Nursing Excellence Party a few months before. We were now solid pals and I really liked her; if I ever wanted anyone to wrestle a hospital administration or tigers on my behalf, it would surely be Angie. "We have a bunch of survivors and donors these days, and we would really like to celebrate them all. The staff wants to do this, and the chief of surgery is willing to support it, so how does your calendar look in early September?"

"Angie, you should know this about my catering service: If I book an outdoor event, it won't rain. Any particular date in September you prefer?"

She laughed at my audacious guarantee that first year, but after five years in a row, she knew we had more than an understanding. She picked the dates, and I guaranteed the weather. It worked for us both.

Over the years her estimates grew from "maybe two hundred?" to "Carol, we're sure to have at least 750," testament to the growing success of organ transplantations. Once we all got over the jokes about liver on the menu, the event drew requests from my staff to be hired to work the picnic. Every guest was there either because they had given an organ, received one, or cared intimately for someone through the interminable waiting and then the long process of readying, receiving, adapting, and healing. Here was the doctor who had taken medical technology leaping into the future and then personally paid for a party to celebrate his victories and thank his crew.

My staff loved working the event. We all knew we would be feeding the homeless park wanderers, giving drinks to the dozens of kids playing ball just at the edge of our tables, and fighting the bees that swarmed around sweet cakes and melons (Anita learned to cut fast, cover quickly, and not get stung!). After the first year, we even learned how to circle the prep tables so no one would steal another roll of my knives or make off with anything more valuable than the food. Everyone in our vicinity at the park was welcome to the picnic.

And we all loved the food! I ordered fried chicken from Pudgie's, made all kinds of pasta and vegetable salads, bought crisp French breads, the best fresh fruit and watermelons Fairway had that morning, cookies and celebration cakes galore. I bought thousands and thousands of chicken parts from Pudgie's, because at the time, they made *the best* fried chicken in town. They could do it safely, we could pick it up just at the time we needed it, and I couldn't have made it cheaper or better myself. Everyone loved it, licked their fingers, and looked forward to getting back on line for seconds.

Year after year, we all enjoyed working that party; it was family. My staff struck up special relationships with different survivors, everyone eager to describe their yearly progress and how much better they were than the year before. I would circulate through the crowd, passing out dozens of handi-wipes, urging people to eat some more, basking in Central Park's sunshine, so glad to be their caterer.

I loved to drive up with the fifteen-foot truck in the mornings. First, I went down to Penske/Hertz Truck Rentals on Twenty-seventh Street and Ninth Avenue, past the hookers coming off duty, to pick up my reserved truck early Sundays.

Then I drove up to Fairway on Broadway and West Seventy-fourth Street for my cases of fruit and watermelon. I stopped to load in my equipment and prepped salads, and to meet my staff. Finally, I tooled up Central Park West, around the top of the Park edging Harlem, past the joggers and dog walkers, past the fishing pond on the northeast corner of the park and then down Fifth Avenue to 103rd Street. I would sing some bawdy sailor's song as we bounced along, and my crew joined in, loud and jolly, out of the back of the rental truck, to everyone's amusement along the street. I backed the truck into a parking space to unload just at the edge of the park outside the Guggenheim Pavilion (where the bathrooms were). We eagerly waited for Tristate Party Rentals to drop off our tables and chairs at precisely 11:00 a.m.; then Diamond Ice dropped off and scooted fast back downtown (just at the edge of Amado's territory, they were gone in a flash!). And, even if it had been overcast up until that point in the day, the sun always broke through just as we were pulling tables and cases of fruit and salads into place. The location seemed ordained after that first year. Everyone knew the bar fit nicely under that tree, the prep staff felt secure with a table behind them up against the tree, several hands rolled the café tables out near the ball field and generated much discussion with those on the field about how much turf we could appropriate that year without our guests getting bopped by fly balls.

Angie and her crew at the Transplantation Division organized registration, brought out the balloons, tee shirts, and posters, and drew on volunteers to solicit organ donations from passers-by. They ate and caroused with patients and families they had nursed and grown close to through those intense crises everyone at these picnics had experienced.

The doctor in charge of the division wrote out his own check to cover expenses for the picnics, and I gave him a price break that would not have been matched by most caterers. It was a winning event all around for five years.

But the politics of the hospital changed. Angie took a job down in New Orleans to create a new transplantation division and open up new venues for her own life. The next administrator asked me for menu proposals and took detailed competitive bids for the picnic, then chose not to have it, since the hospital would not support the effort involved. Just one key person left the hospital, and suddenly no one seemed to remember the joyful pleasure of that annual event. More survivors ensured the ongoing role of organ transplantation to extend human lives, but the gig was over.

Dinner in the Board Room

COMING UP OUT OF THE SUBWAY, my first image of 375 Hudson Street was the classy black façade; it was called the "Saatchi & Saatchi" building. Through black-shaded glass doors, past the security station and into the elevator, I was in a closely monitored corporate building.

I stepped off the elevator to find that Turner Construction Company owned the whole sixth floor. The reception desk sat on the right, and I soon got to see the southwest view across the Hudson River to New Jersey from just below Houston Street, because this was the Big Guy's corner office.

The Corporate Board Room was internal: there were no windows, wainscoting ran up the walls well above my head, and state-of-the-art audio-visual controls were hidden in their own panel, with drop-down screens and door locks controlled from the chairman's seat. If I hadn't known I was on the sixth floor, the room could have been a Hollywood film set for a war room, and years later, it *did* serve as a coordination center for the cleanup following 9/11. The Big Guy had a front-row seat as those planes tore into the World Trade Towers, and Turner Construction played a significant role in the clean-up and in defining the New York skyline thereafter.

But I was there a decade earlier, when corporate secrecy was their concern, LEED "green" construction was nascent, and the men on the board wanted a decent meal, food they could recognize, and the caterer out of the way for their strategic meetings. It was a sensitive job that called for discretion and decorum. I got that immediately.

For several years, Renee C. had provided a basic chicken dinner, but as her third marriage fell apart and that husband battled for her assets, she folded her business and split for her country house. She gave my number to Pat, who called me, explained that Renee had already prepared the food, booked staff to bring it over, and recommended me as cook and quarterback for the board of directors meeting the following evening. Would I do it? She offered me generous compensation for my time, so I wrote down the address and told her, "Sure. I'll be there." I didn't think to mention the cast on my right arm: I didn't want Pat to get nervous. I expected Renee C.'s staff to help me if anything was too unwieldy for me to handle; they had apparently worked the gig before and knew the drill.

I hoped Renee C. was trying to make up to me after having done me dirty a few years earlier, when she promised to rent me her kitchen for a couple of big parties I had booked. The day before I needed to send over my ingredients and equipment, she had changed her mind and would not allow me to work there.

She didn't care to discuss it any further either. My own kitchen was under construction then, and it was a real bitch prepping food for a hundred and fifty people on upended milk crates, the stove plugged into wall studs, sink not yet attached to pipes. *Oh, please,* I had prayed, *don't let the Board of Health find me!*

I had not forgiven Renee C. for that, and we had not spoken since. But I thought perhaps she wanted to make amends, since I *had* helped her get some great press, written up by Elizabeth Crossman in the New York *Post*, when we both catered our own weddings a few years earlier; or perhaps she wanted to encourage me to hire her soon-to-be-unemployed staff—the collegial approach.

But that was totally not the story. The truth was, she couldn't find anyone to pick up her food at the last minute, and my number was still pasted up on her wall, or in her phone book, as she fled the city.

I showed up early the following evening, climbed out of the subway hauling my knives and a few kitchen tools, to have time to check out the kitchen situation, change into my chef's jacket, and introduce myself to Pat. From the reception station at the elevator, I was escorted through back corridors to the kitchen.

Renee C.'s food had arrived, but I didn't see her staff. I took inventory of the technical difficulties in the kitchen, glimpsed the board room, and strolled around the corner to Pat's office. What a view! Her face expressed her shock at seeing my cast, but I smiled at her with confidence. "Hello, Pat, I'm Carol."

"Can you cook like that?" Pat's a straight shooter. I liked her immediately.

"Yes, I'll be fine. I brought along my own tools, the food's all here, and we'll work out the service when I meet her staff. But I think there may be a few technical issues we should talk about."

She made the quick adjustment, shifting her focus from the impediment on my arm.

I had no idea what I would be facing when I first stepped in to finish cooking someone else's food, and coping with Renee C.'s chicken dinner presented quite a few challenges. The stuffed chicken breasts could not be heated in the aluminum containers Renee had sent them in, since there was no oven in this kitchen. There was no pot either in the kitchen large enough for the sauce she had sent in plastic containers. Besides the inadequate size, the pots that *were* there wouldn't work on the brand-new induction heating elements. There was a microwave, and there were Styrofoam plates, a few large plastic spoons, and a salad bowl— corporate-kitchen basics—but nothing that could accommodate the state-of-the-art cooktop, which, of course, took up most of the counter space. I had two square feet to set up dinner for twelve, unless I balanced plates on the cooktop; that gave me just about six square feet.

I explained to Pat how I would be solving these problems. "I'll use your Styrofoam plates to microwave the chicken and sauce in batches, and warm the rice separately with some butter for moisture in that one salad bowl I saw. The beans are already blanched, so I'll just warm them a bit on another plate. Then I'll transfer the food onto the Tiffany china. I don't think it's a good idea to expose that gold leaf to microwaves, so I'm not taking any chances on poisoning anyone, okay? I hope you won't get too many complaints if the food is not really hot when I serve it—this is the best I can do for now."

Pat had little understanding of what I was describing about technique, induction equipment, or food safety, but she got the point: My cast was not the problem.

"Those guys, they came in here, designed the kitchen, the dishes, sold my boss on this whole 'concept,' but you know, I bet they didn't know squat about cooking." She was pissed the earlier consultants had left her with a problem. "Could you buy the right kinds of pots for us? Could you buy whatever you'll need to make dinner for the board's next meeting?"

"Sure," I said. "The pots are available, but it's a bit of an investment. Do you want to authorize a budget or get approvals or something?"

I thought I was being sensitive to corporate protocol, but her scowl told me I was being offensive. "Buy whatever you need and bring me the bill." It was a done deed. She could act with authority in such decisions, and she had just made a few of them. It seemed I would be cooking the next dinner there.

Pat was New Jersey working people: smoking, drinking with the gals, a rough voice and a soft heart, recently single again due to her boyfriend's untimely death, but way too young for the role of widow. Her guy shouldn't have died of a *heart attack!* They were just getting on, making plans, she told me as we got to know one another over the following months. It was a sad tale, but she wouldn't feel sorry for herself. She threw herself into her work, and she was a damned fine administrator—you bet! She told me she had the best boss going, and she was totally protective of him. You could hear Bruce Springsteen singing right behind her. I was Brooklyn, street-smart, and sturdy. There was straight communication between us, and never an issue.

She was the perfect office-wife for a construction company. These fellas handled mega-projects and obviously earned mega-profits; the ones on the board wore hard hats covering conservative heads. It was clearly male turf, and they liked their ladies sassy, spunky, put-together in pearls and pumps. There was lots of cigar smoke at those board meetings. Pat's nails were always done with a rock-hard and shiny surface. Her suits were expensive and impeccable, her manner gruff. She was casual with the office staff, but when it came to her decisions on behalf of her boss, she was quiet, focused, and effective.

I wanted to confirm the implied second gig, so I asked, "When is that next meeting, Pat? Will Renee C. be preparing the food again, like this time?"

"*Pssha!* No way! She flaked out on this job so many times, you wouldn't believe it! Last time she came in, I was out at reception, and by the time I got back here, she was sitting on His desk, giggling, leaning all over Him—would have made you sick! No, you do the food. . .and can you bring your own guys to serve, too? The ones she sends are sloppy and have dirty fingernails. That's not appreciated around here."

I bought the Turner Corporation new pots. We'd talk a few minutes when I arrived, and then I'd stay out of sight in the kitchen. Pat had a fine chicken or salmon dinner served in the boardroom by two handsome, clean, and skilled men, as well as dinner for two at her desk to share with an office mate, served with a glass of perfectly chilled white wine by her favored server, the witty John of the "grand" blue eyes, no extra charge. And *no* one sat on her boss's desk.

We totally understood each other until she called, about three years later, to say the board was economizing with Chinese take-out for their dinners. I always grin when I drive down the West Side Highway, just below the George Washington Bridge, where Turner Construction has kept that section of highway clean for years: Hey, Pat, nice job!

Marcia Lavine's Showroom

MARCIA LAVINE CREATED DISTINCTIVE display furniture to fit limited square footage, and odd spaces in retail shops, for all kinds of merchandise. She enjoyed the design challenges: furniture had to be easy to move, parts had to be interchangeable and as lightweight as Tinker-Toys, total concepts had to be easily assembled with a screwdriver yet sturdy enough to withstand shipping and retail traffic flows, as well as visually stunning enough to meet her standards and the requirements of her clients.

Marcia was as particular about her catering needs as the details of her displays. She had a worldly palate, and she was, needless to say, esthetically exacting. It was fun for me to develop menus with her for the three shows she brought to New York City each year. We talked for hours about each food selection, current food trends, and new products as I gave her New York City foodie updates.

She called me from the wilds of rural Minnesota, where she

lived and where she supervised the construction of her shelving and furniture, but she traveled around the country during the year to sell her products at the major shows for her industry.

In New York City the show was held at the Jacob Javits Convention Center, and it was never easy to work there. The union shop rules meant labor was expensive, and slow at assembling and taking down the yearly shows. Workers seemed to break as many pieces as they handled, which created repair work for another union, which could then guarantee the first union more work moving the repaired pieces a second time.

In disgust, Marcia rented a showroom on West Twenty-seventh Street, near but not in the Javits Center.

To draw clients from the Center to her showroom, she hit upon the idea of feeding the purchasing agents. Food at the Center was generally even more horrible than the usual institutional food service one expected to encounter at a poorly ventilated, filthy convention center, because the problems were compounded by the utter discouragement and outright hostility of the food workers. Their union was constantly locked in unresolved negotiations with the Center management, which had maintained a rather poisonous relationship for a long, long time.

Marcia's strategy was quite successful. She attracted a steady stream of buyers to her space to inspect her products and get off their feet after walking the huge Center, especially around lunch hour. My staff and foods embodied her messages about customized creativity, kind attention, hospitality, and quality. She needed a range of finger foods, luncheons, fruit, drinks, and sweets to attract her buyers while keeping her own staff amused and comfortable through some long, repetitive days.

By the second, certainly the third, day of a show, Marcia's creative staff became bored and frustrated, and they looked for a break from the required politeness and the not-so-subtle pressures to sell. We all got quite friendly over those long hours, joking around out of sight, back in the safety of the tiny showroom kitchen. My crew knew their staff dynamics: We knew who was going to quit when they got back to Minnesota and who was planning to ask for a raise, often before Marcia did. Some mornings, I arrived to learn my staff had taken her crew out dancing and clubbing late into the night, the New Yorkers showing off some flamboyant hotspots to the Midwesterners who needed creative "fueling" for their next six months out in the woods.

Marcia wanted stunning and tasty foods, but she was always concerned that none of our food be messy and damage or stain her display samples. There could be small, single bites of warm puff pastry, treats I purchased from her cousin Judy's business, Dufour Pastry Kitchens.

Judy had initially recommended me to Marcia, so we kept business "in the family." Marsha wanted strong flavors on items that didn't drip, set out with visual panache to perk up her clients' attention. Many sales were pitched over those small plates; the tone of conversations softened with Marcia or my crew urging a tired purchasing agent to taste some morsel, perhaps a chocolate truffle, or sip some really cold white wine or a soft drink. We passed countless immaculate and enticing trays and set out dozens of tempting dishes on the display units, using contrasting floral accents, to demonstrate the flexibility and success of her designs.

I worked many shows for Marcia over several years, but one day I managed to double-book myself to teach a "Careers in the Culinary Arts" class on a Saturday, the week of a show. I already had the menu set and the showroom staffed with my regular crew. Max and Lilia would be there, so I wasn't the least bit worried about the showroom as I spent my day working with adults thinking deeply about life changes.

After my six-hour seminar, as I walked toward the bus home, I entered a phone booth (remember them?) to call the showroom and see whether I needed to pick up anything for Sunday supplies, when I would be at the showroom myself. Lilia got on the telephone, masked the mouthpiece, and whispered, "Carol, something was wrong with the chocolate truffles! When I opened the container Radhica brought over, they smelled *awful!* What happened to them? I didn't serve this batch!"

Those truffles were one of my signature items, and if they were "off," I would absolutely have to prepare another batch for Sunday. But they had never gone bad on me before. "What happened?" I asked.

"Carol, they smelled like *cheese.* I couldn't serve them!"

I was standing on a street corner when my laughter overtook me. In a flash, I saw the containers of both coconut and Parmesan cheese in my freezer. Someone had rolled ten dozen one-inch balls of precious chocolate; had a well-intended employee actually chosen the cheese instead of coconut? How amazing! Thank goodness Lilia knew not to serve them!

I got back to the kitchen and found the empty Parmesan container. I kept laughing and crying as I stirred the expensive chocolate and liqueur into the cream and butter that evening. I chilled the mix and kept right on laughing and crying as I rolled the petite balls in the coconut, glad I had enough to finish the job at 2:00 a.m. It was only money spent, truffles trashed, no one made ill, no client lost.

A day in the life of a caterer, and two lessons taught the teacher: Label everything, and It is possible for *anything* to go wrong.

Mick Jagger's Fortieth Birthday Party

H OW COOL WAS *THAT?* I catered Mick Jagger's fortieth birthday party at the Palladium. Actually, I was a sub-contractor, but still, I played the Palladium! Built in 1927, the Palladium replaced the original Academy of Music, which was across the street. It served New York City as a deluxe movie palace and concert hall, where the Rolling Stones per-formed one of their 1965 concerts and The Band broadcast live in 1976. Steve Rubell and Ian Schrager turned it into a hot club for the City's downtown music scene in 1985, following their extraordinary success with the scene at Studio 54 and before they went to prison for tax evasion on that other property. New York University pulled down the Palladium to build more dorm space near Union Square in 1997; it remains only in architec-tural history books and the memories of those who knew it.

I met a charming woman at several food industry events: Paula was working as Jagger's private chef. Plans for his mid-summer birthday party began to germinate, and Jagger's personal assistant asked Paula to cater it. As a single mother with two daughters to feed, Paula explained to me that she needed money, and that this was an honest way to acquire some. But she had never prepared food for more than twenty people at one time, had no clue about quantities of anything that would be needed for displays and for serving and feeding two hundred guests. She did not have access to staff to work a big event, relationships with ice delivery or rental companies, or insurance for that matter. In short, she was not a caterer, but since they'd asked her, she had agreed and now she was figuring it out.

She made me a proposal: She would handle Jagger's people, create the menu, get the money, shop specialty items, and dip strawberries in chocolate. I would do everything else. She offered me a 50–50 split. She was certain there would be other parties later on as films opened and new records were released. All she needed was a trustworthy catering machine to produce events she would invent, menus she would devise. She was smart; I knew my business, and I thought it would be a hoot to say I had worked for Mick Jagger at the Palladium. It was midsummer, a really slow time for my catering operation, and you never knew what one party could lead to, so I said yes.

As soon as Paula confirmed the party was on, I set to my tasks: shopping, prepping, ordering ice and rentals, booking staff. Everything moved according to her plans: the menu came mostly right off the shelves at Fairway; my kitchen crew cleaned herbs for garnishes, prepped a few dips, and pureed toppings to pipe onto canapés, toasts, and cucumbers. We packed many cheeses, fruit, crackers, and my equipment, and we hauled everything over to the Palladium without unexpected problems. We entered through the huge glass doors of the main entrance to the space on the south side of Fourteenth Street and carried the crates up a broad, dark flight of stairs to the dance floor. Once everything was safely landed toward the rear of the immense space, past the huge old wooden bar, I walked around casing the joint for the first time. While two staff checked the rentals, two others walked with me to determine where to place tables in the available lighting.

Once they had directions to pull together the front of the house, I headed into the makeshift kitchen, which was actually the sound room, toward the rear, Thirteenth Street, side of the building. As I began to open the crates and get my food organized, I heard yelling from the dance space and immediately grew wary and alert: Was my staff in some kind of trouble? Had they moved or broken something? But they were not the problem. Steve Rubell had just fired the ten-piece orchestra. He thundered into the "kitchen," leaped up onto the center set-up table, and walked across, between, and over my trays of foods on his way to his console to change the sound system.

"Ch-*rist*, we are *not* having that bar mitzphah band playing in here! Get another group! *Now!* I'm turning on the tapes." He was not addressing me; he was raging at some assistant I couldn't see. I pulled trays, food, and equipment out from under his plodding, careless boots. Then the band, all of them mature, professional orchestral musicians, slowly and sadly trailed through the sound room, throwing longing looks at the platters of food as they hauled their instruments out the rear door. I certainly couldn't feed them at that point; I could barely protect the food from Rubell's boots. I had not given our own exit a thought until I saw the musicians moving down an external stairway toward Thirteenth Street.

As Paula spun into the sound room in the wake of the exiting musicians, I tried to sound cheery. "What time are we serving until?"

"Well, we're *scheduled* until about 1:00, but if they *want* us to stay on, we will."

"We're opening to the public at 2:00, so just get the hell out of here on time, right?" Rubell growled, glaring at pert, pretty Paula, but his words slid out the side of his face and seemed to hit me. I kept my head down, my hands flying around the cheese trays, pulling them to safety, as Rubell thrashed about, but what was *that* I felt passing between them?

I said, "Sure, fine with me, I'll be packing up as soon as we've set these trays, and I'll just line everything up to exit as fast as we can...." I wanted to sound steady, assuring him of our good intentions, hoping we weren't the next to be sent packing down the back stairs, which I had not actually seen yet. Paula glared back at him. She didn't say a word, just faced him squarely, until he turned his back to her and fiddled with his sound system. He said no more to any of us, and, as he left the room, he jostled my waiters coming in from the dance floor; he was not exactly a charming host.

I sent the staff scurrying with heavily laden silver cheese trays, wicker baskets overflowing with fruits, and assorted tidbits of Paula's menu as quickly as they were set, and we turned the dark, dank dancehall into a stage-set party room. We were ready just when we were scheduled to be: I always tried to run on time, didn't want nervous hosts breathing down my neck, so I let Paula work the crowd and handle Rubell.

For the next few hours, Paula waxed and waned hysterical. Her chocolate-dipped strawberries began to weep in the klieg lights, and I feared she would join them. She needed the attentions of two waiters to carry her stash of tissues around the room, blotting the berries, as she pleaded with the lighting crew to make adjustments. She creased and cuffed the linens and made sure the crackers lined up straight and then curled in a perfect arc to embrace the runny Taleggio. She was wonderful at those fine points: She made sure there were cheese knives and beverage napkins, stacks of small plates and perfectly opened birds-of-paradise in all the right spots, lit for a camera shot, should there be one when the press arrived.

Only the crowd didn't come. Paula had told me to be set at 9:00, so the catering was ready. But no one came at 9:00. No one came at 10:00, and not many were there at 11:00 either, but after that, some famous faces began to show up around the carved oak bar. The music tapes were going; it was loud, I know. Perhaps because I was in the sound room, it was so loud I couldn't tell you what music was played. Rubell didn't come back in, so I figured he and Paula were waltzing around in a game of cat-and-mouse, tacking around the shadows on the dance floor, avoiding or pursuing one another.

When the guest of honor arrived, "Just around Midnight," the first thing we heard in the sound room was Paula's report that Jagger was screaming at Jerry Hall. Hall had just delivered his child, their second or third, and he seemed to be experiencing some post-partem moods. Paula interpreted everything for us: Working as their private chef, she knew the inside scoop. We listened to her tales of a rock-and-roll star's home life, kitchen view. But before the internet, there was such a thing as privacy, and I wasn't quite comfortable hearing her share such information with all the staff. But I was more concerned with watching the clock as it moved inevitably forward, despite Paula's assertive performance before Rubell in the sound room and whatever was happening out on the floor.

The huge, hungry crowds of well-wishers were very late arriving that night, and the only updates the staff could report back to me in the kitchen were about the lines on the bar, the Ludes, the smokes, and the vials passing around the room. The munchies struck a few guests around 2:00 a.m. No, we were not out as scheduled. Paula insisted we leave the party in place long past the agreed-upon time; she would handle it.

"How," I asked, "are we to compensate the staff for the extra time?" Paula had negotiated our price, set the fees, and collected the money in advance.

She said, "Don't worry."

Perhaps she felt the mere wonder of working for Jagger was more than sufficient compensation for her overtime, but I didn't think the waiters felt that way.

The Palladium was scheduled to open to the *public* at 2:00 a.m., so we knew there were throngs of star-spotters, dancers, and revelers crowded by the front entrance, hoping they were themselves beautiful enough for the guards to allow them the privilege of paying for entry, as was the custom at Studio 54. A wilder, screaming mob had also stacked up tight on those back stairs from where the musicians had departed, planning to "crash" the scene, avoid the entrance fee, and reach for a touch of Jagger and the party of the famous into the bargain. But, at 2:00 a.m., I didn't know that.

Close on 3:00 a.m., though the party was just beginning to really swing, Rubell caught Paula out on the dance floor and made it clear we *really* had to get out—*immediately!* So the waiters swept the room, scooped up the same huge, loaded silver trays, right out from under the guests now hovering over them. I caught what I could in the kitchen: instantly sorted the rentals I could identify from my own equipment, emptied all that perfectly good food into trash cans just as fast as six waiters could pull, push, and toss them at me. I rescued silver cheese knives and bagged table linens as fast as my arms could push and my fingers could grasp. The room that had taken over two hours to set up was cleared in less than fifteen minutes.

We stashed the rentals in a corner of the sound room, where they would be picked up in a few hours. My waiters had gathered what they could, covered as much as they could, put out of harm's way as much as they could. Whatever was lost, trashed, or stolen, I would have to pay the rental company for out of whatever profits there might yet be. That was the caterers' relationship with a rental company: If I lost their equipment it was my responsibility to reimburse them for replacement items so they could continue to fulfill their part of the business for me, and so many others.

The waiters had seen what lay before us, although I was still not really getting it, still focused on finding my knives and equipment in those intense minutes. The men gathered around me. They all sensed I was tired; I was coming to the end of working twenty hours straight by then. Each of us had crates of glass bowls or knives in our hands, shouldered our backpacks; most of them were still in their tuxedos, and I was wearing my chef's coat.

One of the waiters asked, "Ready?" Our eyes met—my phalanx of six-footers, tiny Paula, and me. "Hold tight to your personals, everyone," he said, "Here we go."

As the lead three men pushed open those rear doors, we moved against a giant, rising tide of grasping groupies. We were all exhausted physically and off-balance, carrying our packs and the heavy catering stuff, as we leaned onto the waves of people, wearily weaving down the wide and steep, wrought-iron way. I don't know if my feet touched stairs, I doubt it. I don't have a clue who grabbed me, felt me up, or elbowed me down. My bundle and I were shoved along by the capillary action of that over-populated intestine of a horde. They wanted *in*, in the worst way. We wanted *out*, very, very much. Somehow, enough of them passed in to clear space for us to get down and away. The guys got me, and my stuff, into a cab home. Paula disappeared into the crowd.

The next day, she left on a food writing expedition to England. She had told me just before the party began she had been invited to join that junket, so I knew it would be some time before we got to reconcile the financials. I counted up the equipment I needed to replace for myself, and I paid the rental company for what they claimed had been lost. I paid the staff for their extra hours of "combat duty," too.

When Paula returned from England, she brought out her receipts for the huge strawberries, and I showed her my tally of the costs for the rest of the food, so much of it pushed into those garbage cans at the entrance to the sound room.

Paula's eyes grew large in shock at how much we had spent. Obviously, the profit margin was not what she had hoped to see. As for myself, I had truly been burnt by the scene that night and did not venture on such a partnership again. It did not lead to other major parties—but I can honestly tell you I worked for Mick Jagger at the Palladium. . .and how cool was that?

Owning
And Operating

1983–86

Frozen Vodka

A WELL-RESPECTED FOOD JOURNALIST recommended me, just a few days before the end of the year, to cater her friend's New Year's Day open house party. The client, a psychiatrist, called and asked me to meet him the same evening, after his office hours. I gently asked why they had invited eighty friends to their home before thinking of hiring a caterer. He laughed, explained that his wife, a psychotherapist, had been cooking a *cholent*, and the party had grown like Topsy, and, well, sometimes these things get bigger than one anticipates. That sounded reasonable, so we shared the laugh and moved ahead with the plans.

When I asked about renting dishes and cutlery to serve this heavy, East European meat-and-bean dish, he dismissed the idea, waved in the direction of a full wall of built-in closets, and said he was sure they owned plenty of dishes.

We were meeting in a gracious living room on a high floor at the corner of Madison Avenue and Eighty-ninth Street, with views overlooking the Guggenheim Museum and Central Park Reservoir. I saw no reason to challenge his information.

We discussed hors d'oeuvres and finger sweets, the kinds of cheeses he would like, and the need for me to hire two staff, in tuxedoes, to be sure their party would feel well-tended yet not "overdone." He assured me their housekeeper was coming the morning of New Year's Day, and he told me not to worry about beverages as he had already ordered champagne and hired the son of friends to handle the bar. The beverages would be champagne, mimosas, club soda, and frozen vodka. Our rapport was relaxed, direct, and clear. I was glad I didn't have to argue him out of serving red wine with the cholent: I was certain that would be a bad idea for their white carpets.

He expressed no concerns about budget and quickly dashed off a deposit check, with the balance to be paid once I calculated my costs. The conversation moved ahead very smoothly; I thought this would be a lovely start to the New Year among affluent, prestigious guests who would enjoy the party and ask the host for the name of the caterer, opening new business opportunities for my small catering company. It wouldn't hurt that several well-known food writers were expected as guests; I was thinking a nice mention in the press would certainly encourage business.

That night, after our meeting, I calculated what I would charge for this party, typed up our agreement, mailed it to him, and clipped his check to my copy. I was tired and did not look closely at the check. I called a few days later, on December 30, to confirm that everything was in order.

I had worked a very long, hectic Christmas season. I typically did about half my year's work in the weeks between Thanksgiving and Christmas, and sometimes the eighteen-hour days began before the big turkey fest and stretched beyond the holidays into the New Year. It was one of those years: I'd had a terrific fourth quarter but was exhausted and looking forward to the end of this party and some down time to catch my breath, think about spring menus, and plan the next year of my business.

January 1, as I had promised, I arrived early with Thom and Jim, two tall, handsome young men with their tuxedoes, and me with chef's whites, bringing plenty of carefully prepared hors d'oeuvres for the first party of the New Year. The housekeeper opened the door but kept her eyes lowered. She spoke to me only in Spanish as she led me to the dining room, pointed to the table she had set with a perfectly pressed white linen cloth, a stack of ten beautiful, gold-rimmed, hand-painted dinner plates, and maybe a dozen patterned silver forks. I nodded, smiled at her, then asked where additional plates were—but she shook her head. "*No, Senora,*" there were no more. I thought perhaps she hadn't understood why I wanted more plates, but as I followed her back to the hall and pointed to the wall closet the host had indicated to me, she shook her head harder, very clearly indicating I was not to touch things in that closet. Then she grabbed her own coat from the hall closet and left. I had not seen the host or met the hostess yet, so I retreated to the kitchen to get started.

The guys changed into their tuxedoes, and I slipped into my

chef's coat and tied on a clean apron. "Okay, boys, the challenge begins. I have to ask about plates for this crowd, but let's see what she's cooking." I opened the oven, which was still warm and dark inside—there was no light. I needed one of them to haul the heavy cast iron casserole of cholent out and hoist it on top of the stove. I began to set up items to be warmed in sequence, and to arrange the cheese boards.

The host was not available, but his wife eventually came out of the bedroom wing of the apartment. She wanted to explain everything she knew about *cholent*—how long she had baked it, what she had used. She was erudite, an experienced cook, and quite clear about how she wanted her party to run. But when I asked her about additional plates, she dismissed the request with the flick of her wrist. "People will be coming in and leaving all afternoon and eating at different times. Just keep passing hors d'oeuvres, will you? Thanks." And she disappeared again. We would not discuss her concept: She expected us to recycle plates and cutlery as her guests came and went. I looked at the guys, and they looked back at me, grinning. They had taken her measure; we knew we were in for a tough afternoon. I reached into my equipment case and pulled out the long yellow plastic gloves, size large. "We'll take turns," I said.

I turned the oven back on while the guys fanned beverage napkins, placed the cheese boards with tiny champagne grapes and imported Chilean cherries, bowls of my home-made curried cashews, and fragrant, garlicky olives around the living room. We were ready for company. . .except there was no bartender. A small table had been set against one wall, visible as guests came down the entry hall toward the living room. About two dozen glasses were in a box tucked under the table, hidden by the draped, lacy cloth, put there by the housekeeper, I suppose. Jim concluded that this was the intended bar, and we assumed the friend's son bartender would arrive any moment. We were as organized as we could be with food and our service plan. There was some orange juice, club soda, and champagne in the refrigerator, but we didn't find the frozen vodka, and, still, no one was available to ask.

When company began to arrive, the hosts emerged. Jim opened the door and guests handed him their coats, and both host and hostess turned to Thom and simply ordered mimosas for everyone.

"I'll bring them right over to you," he responded. With his dancer's grace, sideways grin, and the finesse he had developed handling the public for years working front-of-the- house in fine restaurants, he came into the kitchen to grab one of my trays and serve the drinks. He opened the champagne and cut in the orange juice. He caught my eye, gave me a knowing smile, and said, "This one is going to be a doozy, Carol."

I nodded, leaned against his shoulder for a breath, and then turned to finish the dill-and-caper garnish on a tray of rose-curled smoked salmon with crème fraiche on pumpernickel, for him to pass.

Jim was stuck at the door as the bell rang repeatedly, busy as LaGuardia's landing strip. The guests assumed he could carry any number of fur coats and simply piled them right up to his chin while they righted themselves. They strolled down the long entry hall, casually asked for a drink at the bar table, where

Thom stepped in to cover, and they joined the party in the living room. Jim at first found hangers and made room in the front closet; then, overwhelmed, he began to pile coats in a bedroom he found off the far wing of rooms. I had warm trays of spinach soufflé-stuffed mushrooms ready to pass, waiting for one of them to get a break, when I began to notice smoke emerging from the oven. I opened a window and closed the swinging doors, trying to prevent the smoke from entering the living room, but for the first and only time in nearly twenty years catering in New York City, just as the party was getting underway, I set off the smoke alarm.

Apparently, the cholent had spilled into the back of the dark oven, and we had not seen that spill when we removed the heavy casserole. As the remains were incinerated on the floor of the oven, they smoked. I had not caused the problem, and there was little I could do at this point to fix it. I had barely warmed the first trays and had several hours of party to go. Thom was the quickest to respond: He kicked off a shoe, stepped up onto a chair and pulled the batteries out of the alarm. Jim propped open the hall door, one of the swinging kitchen doors, and all the kitchen windows. They had the kitchen aired out about a minute before my red-hot rage became audible. I was so angry and humiliated: This was not the signature of my elegant catering service.

Of course, it had happened just as a famous, sharp-tongued food writer strolled in. There are few people who would berate someone caught under such circumstances, but she was definitely one of them. I imagined her snide headlines, guaranteed to ruin any future business I hoped to generate: "This Caterer

Will Smoke Your Apartment, Not the Salmon," "Caterer Serves Icy Blasts for a Very Chill Winter Event," "Frozen Party, Smoky Smells," "Find Your Own Plates, but Smoke Will Find You."

The guys came into the kitchen to get me past my hissy-fit and focused again. They made a few jokes while they bussed several of the dinner plates. "Carol," Thom barked, "put on those gloves and get these plates back on the table—the food critic is heading for the dining room. Come on, stop yer sniveling!"

Swallowing my fury was hard, but I kicked back into gear with the oven door open, burning off the remains of the *cholent*. I stood at the sink, shivering in the January breeze, as the smoke cleared. I tried not to listen to the not-so-subtle living room comments, "Oh, I bet your caterer made a mess in the oven, tee-hee-hee!"

When we were about an hour into the party, the rooms were full, noisy, and no one was choking on the smoke anymore. We had settled into a fast, rhythmic pace: Thom served drinks and passed hors d'oeuvre trays in the living room, Jim bussed dinner plates right out from under guests' noses to hustle them back into the sink and take another tray of hors d'oeuvres to the dining room while I washed and dried the dishes and cutlery, and reset a tray of hors d'oeuvres. Thom brought in empty glasses, grabbed another hors d'oeuvre tray, stopped to serve at the bar, and passed the tray; Jim brought in more plates, reset the dining room table, and was bringing in more glasses when a frazzled teenager showed up: not much beard but total distress showing among the pimples popping on his face.

Since he had rushed directly into the kitchen, not stopping

to remove his coat, and planted himself right in the middle of the six-foot-square space, we suspected he might not be one of the guests. Jim spoke first. "Hello, there—what can we do for you?"

The kid was panting hard. He had been running. "I was waiting for the vodka to freeze! It just didn't freeze!" He was distraught and confused as he pulled the liter of vodka out of its paper bag. It was cold alright, but he would not have achieved frozen vodka for another millennium: Martha Stewart had taught some of us to "freeze" vodka by placing a liter in a half-gallon milk carton filled with water, decorated with a rose. When the outer container was removed, the vodka would be encased in ice. The kid did not know that, though, and since he was about sixteen, he might not have known much about 80-proof anything.

While the host might have thought it a nice gesture to hire him, for this teenager to be shopping, transporting, and serving liquor at a party in the good doctor's home was very much against New York State law. Had anyone stopped the boy en route to the party, or any guest gotten into trouble drinking too much, I doubt the police or my insurance company would have blamed the host. It would have been so easy to sue the caterer, to transfer responsibility to "someone else."

Jim patted the kid on the shoulder, sympathized with his good intentions, and took his coat. I stuck my head back into the oven to pull out more hors d'oeuvres.

Thom wrapped the young man in an apron and introduced our system of bussing used glasses and plates into the kitchen, so I could wash and send them out again. Then he safely opened the champagne bottles in the kitchen and handled the rest of the bartending. We needed the young man's hands, and my guys supported whatever effort he was able to make. Better than the housekeeper, at least he was *present*.

I washed those dinner plates at least eight times each in the next three hours: I know the pattern only too well. I washed every glass so many times I lost count, and broke none. My yellow gloves were trashed well before the end of the party, and the skin on my hands was peeling and purple, as the water supply sputtered hot and cold with the afternoon demands of lower floor apartments. We served lots and lots of hors d'oeuvres.

When I finally did look closely at that first deposit check, it was dated the middle of January into the New Year: it could not be deposited until two weeks after the event. And when I finally billed, called, and sent a second bill reminder for the balance of payment, which I had to go retrieve (stamps cost the good doctors too much?), that check was also from out of state, and it took another month to clear. I had bought the food, paid my staff, and covered all my costs of doing business. I carried the expense of that party for almost two months afterwards, which was not a stellar practice for any small business. The party did not generate my hoped-for new business, of course, but at least I did not see the horrid headlines I imagined.

I had been hired by masterful manipulators and desperately wished there was a way for caterers to check out the people who intended to hire them. I want to review and rate *host* behaviors, but all these years later, that app has not yet been created.

Dinner for Four

ANDY ALWAYS DID THINGS HIS OWN WAY. He was a big, lumbering guy with a graying beard and longish hair. Once you met him, you knew he never stayed within the lines or followed the rules. He was miles ahead of the Harvard Business School, had skipped through their Executive Weekend Program. He was a competitive and creative self-made entrepreneur, and he loved his New York City life and all the people and adventures he found there. He talked to everyone, driven by curiosity and fueled by the city's high-energy demands. He was one of my favorite clients and favorite New Yorkers ever.

He had just bought an incredible penthouse apartment—actually three apartments—overlooking the East River, wrapping around the south, east, and western sides of the building. I don't know how the co-op board allowed him to buy all three, but he had enough money to pay everyone's prices.

I had catered several parties for his company and his daughter's birthday celebrations before he asked me to prepare a very elegant dinner for four. He had invited his wife and their best friends to meet at the penthouse spaces he had just purchased. The interesting part of the assignment, as Andy presented it to me, was that the kitchen appliances, all the personal furnishings, and the light fixtures had been removed by the prior owners. He wanted me to rent a table and four chairs, candelabra, and linens. "Bring one of your guys in a tuxedo— Max would be nice—and you figure out how to cook a really elegant dinner there. See ya Thursday."

That was about as specific as his directions ever were: sometimes he would tell me where he wanted the company party, and sometimes he asked me to find a new and offbeat location; sometimes he would ask for a favorite food, but mostly he liked to see how I could surprise him.

I thought about the menu a while and, by Wednesday afternoon, decided I should stick to a classic. I had called in the rental order and talked to Max, to be sure his tuxedo was clean. I did not think white gloves were necessary, but he could bring them anyway. Thursday morning, I packed my hotplate, cooked wild and basmati rice with shallots, thyme, and buttered pecans (so they would just need to warm); I chose pots I could stack up for steaming, poured some wine into a plastic container to transport safely, and picked the herbs. I knew I would be poaching salmon by the light of a bare kitchen bulb, so I packed an extra bulb, along with extension cords. I would melt dill butter on top of the salmon at service and lay it next to the warmed rice and those darling steamed baby vegetables. Max would pass some cold hors d'oeuvres beforehand, and I had baked apple tartlets, fine at room temperature for dessert with a dusting of confectioner's sugar. Then I would boil water for tea or pour through filtered coffee as they were finishing the entrée: It was simple and elegant, all balanced behind a closed door on upturned milk crates.

Hey, I thought myself clever, serving a hot dinner without kitchen appliances. Max acted the butler role to perfection. The pure white table linens draped to the floor, chilled champagne and chardonnay set in standing coolers, the fragrance of the warm, rich dinner by candlelight: Max and I thought it was to die for.

The dinner went smoothly, all consumed, right down to the final *petit fours* I always made, and I envied Ellen her caring, romantic husband, offering this elegant evening to warm their new home before the renovations began. At the end of the evening, Andy came in to thank us. "Carol, Max, you guys gave me exactly what I wanted, without my even describing what I wanted!" He had enjoyed everything.

But he seemed dejected nevertheless. I asked what was wrong, and he confessed, "Ellen doesn't like the place. She wants to move to New Jersey, have a house for the kids, and let them grow up in the suburbs. I thought I would convince her that this could be a wonderful lifestyle as well, but she doesn't like it."

Families have to make hard choices. With both adults working overtime, a full-time nanny, and a housekeeper, it sure seemed to me to be a shade easier to live in Manhattan and save on commuting time, but Ellen had a different idea.

Andy prevailed—they renovated the apartment, moved in with lots of wonderful customized architectural details, and once the kitchen counters were in place, I catered many Super

Bowl parties, everyone's birthdays, and grandparents' anniversaries for years afterward. I was in their kitchen for many life celebrations, always greeted with kisses by the nanny, guests, and grandparents. Andy had brought me from our initial business contact as his company's caterer into his private circle of family and friends.

Then, just before the kids hit their teens, he sold his business. Ellen quit her high-powered job and joined her family's business, and they moved to New Jersey. Andy was working from home, planning a new venture to sell advertising in space, on something to be called the "internet," several years before e-commerce was a common term in our language.

He was also heading into the hospital to have his gall bladder removed. He seemed subdued, a bit on the quiet side, but claimed he was getting adjusted to suburban life. He rarely went outside, where his allergies bothered him too much, and he rarely got into the City, what with kids' soccer games and such, but he was excited about his new business venture. The kids seemed happy, Ellen was happy, so he was making the best of it, finding his way into the suburban lifestyle.

I learned months later that Andy had died in the hospital. Septicemia is an unusual cause of death in a modern hospital, but just a few miles west of New York City he developed an infection, spiked a fever, and died. He was forty-eight years old. Ellen buried him privately, so friends only learned of his death from other friends. I never heard again from Ellen, so I guess the kids grew up in the suburbs, as she wanted, and for her I had just been hired help she left behind in New York.

New York Road Runners Club:
It's Just Business

THE WIND IS COLD, THE GRAY CHILL WHIPS the dead brown leaves down the streets, the banners are up again, and it's time for another New York City Marathon Race. But now I can skip town—avoid the traffic, the travelers, and the spectacle. I have no need to worry thousands of details; I can chuckle. I can cook a small pot of soup. My skin is dry, but this year it's not cracked to bleeding. I am not working for the Club this year, but for five years I did.

Yes, I fed them: the dozens of homeless men taken from the shelters on flatbed trucks to paint blue racing lines across twenty-six-plus miles of city streets, to set up barricades against the pressing crowds, and to hang banners, flailing in the wind, off the street lamps; the yuppies, hoping to meet "someone" across a computer screen or scouting the displays of the newest style racing shoes; the corporate executives who volunteered, for so many reasons, and always let me know that they were

Leaders. To me, they were all hungry people seeking a friendly face, trying to soothe a frustration, or hoping to warm up after hours outside, working on cold and windy streets.

For the week before the Marathon, the New York Road Runners Club occupied the basement level of the Sheraton Hotel, which my catering crew entered from Fifty-second Street. The Club booked a number of suites and rooms upstairs for the elite marathon runners arriving from around the world. I never got to see the elite runners since they were waltzed around town, interviewed by the sports press, and occupied signing the commitments for financial endorsements to follow a race win. But for the unknown volunteers, the paid recruits, and the backbone staff of the Club who actually made the race happen, my small catering company put out about three thousand meals in five days.

The race was a monumental feat of organization. The New York City Marathon was the largest, best-funded, and best-known running event in the world in the 1980s.

I had the chance to do wonderful work that I loved, feeding hundreds of people. I knew the military precision needed to bring all the elements together, and the overwhelming tasks everyone performed, to play their parts. I was seduced by the power of our ability to organize, create, serve, and help to build the New York City Marathon; everyone could see it was growing larger each year. My catering staff shared the swelling pride as our small team contributed to the Big Event, the human project beyond the capacity of any one person, which culminated in the ultimate achievement of a single person to win *the race!* Hundreds of people contributed small tasks, piece by piece, to make it happen. It was wonderful to participate; our work gave each of us the chance to feel the intense, powerful charge of people working together on a huge, peaceful task. *And* we earned a good week's pay. It was joyful and great!

But by the time the sleek athletes were skipping out across the span of the Verrazano Bridge, my catering marathon was done. Most years I was too tired to take a place at the finish line, to welcome those world travelers who had coursed through the five boroughs. I never marked my mileage; I never timed my hours across distance. I did time each delivery, though, each staff shift and my production schedule. I kept the Club's crews and volunteers fed as they enrolled 20,000 then 23,000, then 28,000 runners, as each year the race grew in popularity and registration, with more and more lucrative awards and sponsorships, drawing national, then international, media attention. I never went to the finish line or the big pasta feast, sponsored by Ronzoni, which was making pasta over in Queens for the last century. The camera crews went there on Saturday night, just before Sunday's big race. That was when I got home to wash up everything from the week's chaos, to clean and store away my stainless pans, check for lost and broken equipment, and rub cream into my stiff, bruised hands. Sunday, as the runners braced themselves against the elements, pushed the limits of their individual endurance, and were finally wrapped in their silver thermal victory blankets, I lay collapsed on my bed, wrapped in a haze of details, food quantities, and notes for next year, recovering and deeply exhausted, prone through the hours of the race.

Initially, a friend who ran with the Club gave my name to Muriel. "Pat says you're the caterer for us!" So we met, if you call it a meeting. I went to the New York Road Runners Club headquarters on East Eighty-ninth Street and found a torn leather chair outside an office, between some boxes, on a landing between the first and third floors of the grand old townhouse.

A skinny, gray-haired dude loped by, looking preoccupied, dressed in jogging cloths, glasses half way off the bridge of his nose. He barely glanced at me. Thus did I meet Fred Lebow, the Club founder, endowment fund, and leader. Then Muriel arrived in a halo of platinum waves, leopard-patterned clothes, and heels high enough to cripple any runner.

"Hello!" She wanted everyone to know she was there. The Club was a noisy and tumultuous place, but you could have heard her in Bangkok. We moved into a room with boxes stacked high along the walls, people coming and going searching for items or papers, asking, "Did you see. . . ?" as she explained my services would be needed in the back of the Sheraton Hotel basement to feed an unknown number of workers three meals and snacks for five days before the race. Was I interested?

"Of course, but there may be a small issue." I began to explain to her that the Sheraton was a union shop, and that there could be significant objections to my presence. My small catering business was not unionized. She was asking me to cross a union line, and I thought this had the potential to grow ugly.

"Oh, no, no, no, dear, there is nothing like that going on! We do it all the time. Everyone makes allowances for us."

Over the next years, I learned just how many allowances

that included. New York City laws, police regulations, and social etiquette were "adjusted" to accommodate the New York Road Runners Club. After the first marathon, apparently, I was approved, and so I worked many races and Club events. I was handed live wires from lampposts in the middle of Central Park, so I could plug in my coffee urns and brew hot coffee for breakfast runs. I saw New York City streets and Central Park roadways closed down for races, with and without police protection. I was asked to cook for hundreds in a church kitchen while mass was being served upstairs, and I was asked to heat food over Sterno and boiling water when open flames were not permitted, so crossing a union line didn't rate as even a minor issue for the Club. I learned to slink past the union haulers, and to grease palms as my staff pulled cases off our van. And when it turned out that one of my staff had dated one of the Sheraton haulers back in high school, well, my catering company gained several dollies (a major corporate asset for me at the time) to more easily move our stuff in and out of office buildings for many years to come.

At our first and only actual meeting, Muriel swore she was very, very good at procuring all kinds of foods, so the budget didn't have to be very big. She would supplement my menus with all kinds of things, she said. She knew everyone, and between her contacts and Fred's we would have *so much food*, she said. So all she wanted me to do was to prepare the basics; she would fill in with all sorts of things. What, exactly, those items would be, she couldn't tell me. That would depend on what the corporations contributed; but I should not even think about paper goods, drinks, or snack foods, since Coca-Cola (and consequently Frito-Lay) were big supporters. She couldn't give me an exact budget either, but she would let me know, she said.

I drew up pretty basic menus to maintain a really tight budget, somewhere around $10–12,000 for the week that first year, and I never heard complaints about my invoices. As this "fluid procurement" relationship evolved, I estimated I was given about $3.25 per person as a food allowance to provide peanut butter, jelly, bread and butter, fresh fruit, cake and cookies, hot coffee, tea and Sanka (contributed) from 7:00 a.m. through 9:00 p.m. for five days running, for several hundred people each day.

And then, there was to be breakfast, lunch, and dinner. In case you haven't purchased food for athletes in a while, even wholesale, even basics, this was a tight budget for New York City in the mid 1980s.

The contributions arrived according to some mysterious schedule never made clear to me. When foods did materialize, I served them, but they did not cut down the quantities I needed to have on hand, prepared. I worked five marathons and can remember six cases of iceberg lettuce arriving one day, delivered to the basement of the Sheraton, where I had no refrigeration, so salad was prominent on the menu the next few meals. I remember four cases of McIntosh apples arriving another time, but the runners demanded more bananas!

When the work teams were released for a fifteen-minute break, coming cold and hungry off a line-painting truck, I had to have hot food available. Whatever the contributions were, they were not a hot, cooked meal, and they rarely appeared when they were most needed. Sometimes Al, the floor manager (the General of Operations), let me know the crews would be arriving in ten minutes; sometimes the men just arrived, hungry.

Breakfast ran into lunch ran into dinner. Snacks were available all the time. It was constant feeding, like Morrison's Cafeteria or some hospital food service operating around the clock. I wanted every person coming through that line to receive a smile, a kind word, and eye contact along with food. When a homeless man extended a plate and asked permission —permission!—to take a second slice of bread, I couldn't help myself and slapped three more onto his plate, and scooped butter on top for him while my staff, next to me, ladled the hot food and understood my idea of "portion-control" for this crowd. When the pissed-off yuppie complained, "Meatloaf, again?" I politely pointed out that it was a fine homemade country pate she was refusing, the most expensive item I was serving all week, and again offered her a slice. When the big man wearing glasses, his shirt open under his suit revealing a Superman T-shirt, wanted to discuss various meals he had enjoyed around the world as relief from the tedium of sorting out computer errors, I put down the serving spoon, and we talked: I shared a few intimate tastes from my youth, a night in Fiesole, overlooking Florence, the wine, the sunset, the pasta, the architect from Philadelphia. . . .

This was the time of Three Leslies in my life. I was already married to Leslie Mark Wertheim (and we were figuring that out). I was renting the catering kitchen of Leslie McBride, of Carroll/McBride Catering (she repaid my loan, remarried, and relocated—where are you, Leslie?) and Leslie Revsin, chef, Michael's boss, and my friend (we negotiated Michael's schedule that week so he had mornings to prep with me and could then run over to his job on her kitchen line a few hours later than his normal shift). Michael could handle the prep for three hundred simple dinners almost single-handedly, with one or two staff I hired to keep him company, wash those fresh veggies, and send them along to his chopping station as fast as he was ready for them. It was an efficient kitchen, with the prep person cleaning up after Michael split for his real job. Leslie McBride came back into her kitchen for her own evening events, with room still available in her walk-in, so we were a good complement to her business and I could hand her some extra cash for using her space that week.

My dad retired the week before our first marathon in order to help me. He drove my van for pick-ups and deliveries: At 5:00 a.m. he started in from Brooklyn with Mom; they picked up muffins, bagels, or pastries from Voilá downtown, on their way across the bridge, then met me at Fairway on the Upper West Side by 7:15 a.m. to load in the cases of fresh fruit and veggies Harold and David sold me at wholesale prices, then drive to the Sheraton. Dad delivered me and Mom, pastries and fruit, by 7:30, then continued on to take the vegetables down to the West Village kitchen.

I was a fixture at the Sheraton, until closing time at 9:00 p.m. I started my morning busily setting out baskets of fresh fruit, bagels, or pastries. The first night, someone from the Club wanted coffee, plugged in one of my hundred-cup urns, and forgot about it; this burned out the empty pot. By the second morning, I had learned to fill the urns at night, and I paid Lianne or Lilia to start the coffee urns at 6:30 a.m., before they went to their office jobs, so the Club managers were usually into their second cup by the time I arrived with breakfast, and we would have a quick "touch base" before the day got rolling. They'd fill me in on juicy fragments of gossip and the disasters *du jour*. I learned which elite runners had been injured on a training run, what had been stolen from the secured spaces, what scandal hushed up by Sheraton managers about the drinking and "escorts" in the hotel rooms.

By the time Dad got to the kitchen downtown, around 8:00 a.m., the prep staff was already slicing cold cuts for the hero sandwiches on Zito's loaves, purchased from the bakery just around the corner, the water was up in huge vats for rice, pasta, or couscous, and sometimes a soup had been started for lunch or dinner. Dad dropped off the vegetables and then headed over to the Bowery. In addition to a coffee urn, we lost serving spoons constantly and would need another half dozen to get on with dinner that night. He went over to Yavarkovsky's on Ludlow Street, where "the old lady" always sat at her desk wearing her black mink coat (no matter the weather!). She knew exactly what inventory she had in her warehouse *and* exactly what I had bought the last time I came in for paper goods months earlier. Dad picked up more napkins: The dozens of cases in the "contributed" supply were suddenly gone.

We didn't have cell phones (or walkie-talkie devices) in the 1980s, so I had to relay messages through a variety of volunteers and Club staff, then double-check whenever I could get to a phone booth to confirm changes and messages through my kitchen crew. Dad picked up whatever we needed and was back at the kitchen for 10:00 a.m. lunch pick-up. Then he drove through the midtown traffic that intensified each day of the week, building as the Marathon crowds came to town, to return to the Sheraton entrance on Fifty-second Street before 11:00 a.m. Someone from the Club would let us know he was outside, my staff and Club volunteers would race to unload whatever was coming off the van before the police chased Dad off, and I would try to pass him instructions on what he needed to pick up next, before he went back downtown to the kitchen to pick up dinner. Whoever was working my morning crew usually had to leave by 11:00 a.m. to work their restaurant kitchen jobs for another ten- or twelve-hour shift, so I was always praying for the next shift to arrive on time. I needed those reinforcements! Sometimes my key crew member was Mom, who so enjoyed licking spoons full of the fresh Bazzini peanut butter straight out of industrial #10 cans: Watching her made everyone smile. We passed the day, in our small, curtained space, chopping salads, setting out bowls of condiments from gallon glass jars, keeping the buffet baskets full of breads, pastries, and fruits, and constantly refilling the paper goods. I think they ate the napkins.

Mom loved to talk with the fascinating cross section of our society. At the time, it seemed as if everyone in the world was running and happy to stop and talk with us. When Muriel swung by on those stiletto heels, I tended the tuna salad while Mom engaged her, so I would not get in her face about the contributions that never arrived.

The dinner drop-off was somewhere around 4:00 p.m., and usually by then Mom was pooped, so I sent her home with Dad on the van, hoping they would come back again the next day— good help was so hard to find! The prep kitchen was finished by then, so my next service shift might be one of the prep cooks, riding uptown with the food on Dad's van, for the extra pay. Sometimes I recruited a gym teacher or other friends eager for runners' swag and the adrenalin rush, with an hour or two between their day jobs and evening social events. Sometimes actors, between auditions, were the crew I cobbled together for that late afternoon shift. Often that was when I realized I needed to step out to the bathroom, and *someone* had to be at the food station.

Dinner buffet was hot and ready from about 4:30 p.m. until 9:00. We set up the Sterno, our deepest six-inch hotel pans with simmering water from the coffee urns, then four-inch pans of food, with two-inch pans held as the last back-up portions for the latecomers. We heated pasta with sautéed fresh veggies, sometimes chicken and sausage with peppers and onions, pasta with Italian "gravy," ziti with and without meat, vegetarian lasagna, and pounds and pounds of sliced meatloaf. We offered couscous with butternut squash and beef tagine (yes, in the 1980s that was unusual and exciting for mass feeding!), mixed bean salads, pans of *spanakopita*, freshly made new potato salads with herbed vinaigrette (not mayo!), bowls of bread-and-butter sweet pickles and salty gardiniere, cheese boards, and crackers with grapes and cut oranges, and lots of fresh green salad with vinaigrette dressing—as much variety, quantity, and great quality as I could afford on tight budgets and still pay the bills, staff, and myself.

Sometime during the evening, my husband would drop by to visit. It was his only chance to see me vertical that week, and the only chance to encounter dinner, of any sort, with me. If he was energetic, or liked the other crew members on the shift, he would hang out until closing time; otherwise, he found something more pressing to do at home. I don't think he liked serving food to hundreds of strangers as much as I did.

The 5:00–9:00 p.m. slot was always the biggest hit of the day. Volunteers came after days at their office jobs to help register runners throughout the evening, and their compensation was our dinner. We were feeding the homeless men at the end of their cold, hard work day, the Club staff, and full-day volunteers bored and tired from long hours of question bombardment, who needed a break before continuing to work into the evenings. Any number of Sheraton workers stopped by to eat as they wandered through the basement hauling merchandise, hooking up electric and computer lines, and sweeping for freebies. I guess our dinners were more appealing than hotel staff meals, an unexpected perk. Feeding maintenance staff sure helped to get the fuses fixed fast when the coffee urns drew too heavily on our "dedicated" electric lines. In five years, we didn't cause any union confrontations, as I had initially feared, and our food was useful for the General to barter favors.

Later in the evenings, as the number of customers tapered off, I made one last pass around the floor to make sure all the managers had given everyone a dinner break, and to let everyone know the coffee would be cut off soon. After the first night's burn-out, we reset the three big urns at a slop sink, deep in the Sheraton basement, behind a blue-cloth screen. I left the pots set for the morning, but sometimes a midnight Club crew member would come prowling with the munchies. My 6:30 a.m. staffer would then find long-brewed, scorched coffee, milk spoiled on the table, and food we thought had been wrapped and hidden away for the next day's menu gone. Dad would have some extra stops added to his schedule, after we checked in at the morning drop-off, but at least the coffee urns survived! Al would see the damage wrought overnight and, during our morning meeting over that second cup of coffee, authorize me to buy more foods, replace lost and broken equipment, anything to keep me happy. He had been in the military as well as the civil service, and he fully appreciated the old maxim: Can't march an army on an empty stomach. When his troops were happy with the food, all other problems could be solved. He wanted to keep me happy because I kept his troops happy. We worked well together those five years, and I felt I was part of the team, called in on short notice when they may have been short in funds, but there was definitely straight talk, cooperation, and respect, the underpinning that made tough work easy.

Each year, Muriel would call me. "Hello, *dahling!* It's me, Muriel! Are you good for the Marathon this year?" and the next year, "Hello, *dahling!* We gonna see you at the Sheraton again this year? We got great chips already at the Club! Fred's talking to so many corporate sponsors, I just know we'll have a lot of goodies this year!" and the next year, "Hello, my friend! We had a great event over the summer, and everyone is looking forward to this year's Marathon. What new will you offer on your menus?"

And then, after I handed in my proposed menus for the sixth year, still worked out within a tight budget, Muriel didn't call me. We didn't get around to the conversation promising contributions as we had for five years.

Al notified me of "budget constraints." Things had changed: The Club had taken my menus to restaurants and asked several to provide one or another of the meals I proposed for free. Muriel was busy working on more contributions, he said, so we never really got to say goodbye. At least Al looked me in the eye, shook hands, and the General gave me a hug, but it was just business.

I had a different gig the following November. Guess I had learned what I was supposed to know about Marathon feeding.

Park Avenue Duplex

N O TIP! I PAID YOU!" "Yes, you paid me for the catered
event—but staff, just like waiters in a restaurant, earn
gratuities if their service was excellent. It is the usual
and customary way this is handled. Don't you think my staff
worked hard tonight?"

"I *paid* you!"

Staff were moving my gear out of the apartment, sweating
at the end of the long night, after endless rounds up and down
the grandiose curved staircase, carrying trays, cleaning after
themselves and guests, careful of the precious Kashmiri carpets,
the Louis XV antique furnishings, Limoges china, and Lalique
crystal glassware. With the French doors swung open for the
guests to easily access the evening air on the upstairs wrap-
around penthouse balcony, the air conditioning indoors was
useless. My staff moved upstairs, outside, and downstairs
through several living rooms and the twenty-six-foot-high ceil-
inged central hall for five hours, in full tuxedos. Each one must

have clocked at least thirty round trips back through the kitchen. The "easiest" gig was bartending: standing, bending, turning, pouring, wiping up, and restocking ice while stationed out on that sun-warmed balcony, after hauling everything up the staircase. There was a great panoramic view to the east, south, and west of New York City, if the staff had a moment to enjoy it. Although I was in the kitchen, I knew my crew had worked hard all evening. Didn't the hostess?

"Was there anything wrong with their service this evening? Was anything damaged, or anyone rude to your guests? Did you lack for anything you requested? Were Mr. S.'s needs met? Was his nurse treated well?" I tried to make her see how you don't notice the service when it's really good. It's just done: no fuss, no one uncomfortable, no one asking again and again for something, no irritations or concerns for guests or hosts.

"No, I paid you!"

"Step back." Bobby, a regular by then, was at my elbow, whispering just below her hearing level. "Carol, let it go, she's not going to budge, and the evening will end badly—she'll never hire you again. Let it go." He pointed at our equipment, so she might think he was questioning my direction to take our leave.

"Okay, Bobby, let's take everything out, carefully. Thank you." I nodded quietly to him. He had rescued me from my temper, once again, my Waiter God. We would leave. These were some of the wealthiest people I had ever worked for, owning fabric mills down south. The host was a self-made millionaire, but aging now, frail and dying. She was frightened and facing imminent widowhood; so little seemed under her accustomed control. Perhaps control over a gratuity was really more important to her than the dollars would be to me.

"Thank you, Mrs. S. I hope you enjoyed the party and will have a good snack tomorrow—I left lots of food in your refrigerator!"

"Well, I'll have to have the children come over to finish it all up!" she whined: It seemed an imposition I had placed on her.

"The rental company will come on Monday and remove everything from the back stairwell. Sylvia supervised our kitchen clean up, so I know you won't find anything amiss there. Have a good rest tomorrow, and I hope Mr. S is feeling better, with a good night's sleep. Good night." I kept my voice level, but I was burning with rage.

The building elevator operator, professional although obviously warm in his full livery, delivered me to street level. When I emerged from the wood-paneled, mirrored elevator, I had peeled out of my chef coat and appeared in my T-shirt and jeans when I reached the street. I faced the waiters, standing guard over my equipment at the curbside. I had checks for each one of them to cover their scheduled hours; gratuities I usually handed out in cash.

"We'll get you a cab, Carol. Do you need a hand unloading at the other end?"

I always had that courtesy offered by one or more of my guys. No matter how exhausted they were, someone always made sure to take care of me, often Bobby.

"I think you all really busted your butts tonight. She was a bit of a jerk at the end. I know how hard a gig this was." I reached deep into my pocket and peeled off extra bills for each one of them. It had to come from me; these men had carried me through the hot night, and they would come out and carry me through many more. Some call it gratuity and think it is optional, but I know they earned a thank-you beyond the wages promised. Why didn't she see that?

When she called me to cater again (thank you, Bobby!), I built gratuity into my price, so she believed she was in control and I could appropriately thank my staff. But I was growing tired of such games with customers who could well afford to tip my staff.

I WAS BACK IN THAT PARK AVENUE duplex penthouse several times; each event I worked was taxing. The most fun was when the hostess offered her apartment to a friend to celebrate her father's hundredth birthday. The extended family, thirty-five guests in all, gathered, and I thought such a celebration at the end of a long life would be a wonderful capstone to my catering experiences.

I went to the apartment, exchanged a friendly hello with Sylvia in the kitchen as I waited to meet the friend, who appeared as an elegant *grand dame*, dressed in a formal light blue silk suit. She bore a striking resemblance to Queen Elizabeth. She knew exactly what she wanted: She even handed me the recipe for the *paella* she wanted me to execute, although the recipe was to feed six. She assumed there would be no problem for me to increase the quantities for her thirty-five guests. The hostess knew I worked carefully and left a clean kitchen behind;

she had a well-stocked kitchen, there was no need to bring my own pots, she assured me. The friend wanted to keep the price moderate, with just two service staff, because Sylvia would be in the kitchen to help, she assured me. She gave me the date, the time, the menu, the recipe, the deposit, and a quick goodbye; she would order the birthday cake her father loved. On my way out of the building, not quite fifteen minutes after arriving, I thought how little negotiation had taken place for this new client, but the hostess trusted me not to wreck her home, and it was understood between the friends that I was "her caterer."

As soon as I got home I booked Max and Millie to help with the event. They both knew the apartment and liked working together. Their rapport would make my afternoon a pleasure, and the event would run smoothly.

I thought *paella* an interesting choice for the celebration and would have loved to ask a few questions, as that classic Spanish dish clearly held some significance in the elderly gentleman's life. I was delighted to catch sight of him slurping up seconds when Millie pressed open the kitchen door, carrying a refilled platter to the buffet table. He was all tucked in with napkins at his collar and across his lap in the wheelchair, only paying attention to the movements of the spoon arriving before his face. His daughter, grandkids, and great-grandkids were all buzzing around him, cracking lobster shells, waving shrimp held by their tails at one another, while Millie and Sylvia took turns spooning yellow rice, pimentos, shelled lobster bits, and spicy sausage into his wide open, eager mouth. I was so glad to be their caterer that day.

Max served the buffet and tended bar while Millie worked at the table, refilled the buffet, and cleared. She had worked several parties with me in that apartment, so the families knew her, and she could properly pronounce *paella*. In her real life, Millie was a petite firecracker, an actress and mother of two girls. While we set up, she talked about her strategies to keep her husband contributing to the family's support and engaged in their relationship. She worked catering gigs between auditions, when she could get them, and she was a reliable server for me for many years. She figured out how to work the dishwashers and where the silver had to be returned; she folded the linens precisely and checked to see there was a stack of beverage napkins close at hand without needing a reminder. I could send her out independently, and I trusted her to clean up the kitchen and leave the silver.

When the Grand Dame started to whine, in the middle of this *paella* party, "Heavens, I can hardly find the rice!" Millie sassed her,

"Well, it's better that way than complaining you can't find the shellfish!"

That brought a laugh around the table—and then Millie came into the kitchen, sputtering with exasperation. It pissed her off to hear these very wealthy people find something to complain about, but she knew she had to keep cool in front of the party and let off her steam among the pots and pans. This was an important distinction, and the etiquette I wanted in my crew.

I sent out batches and batches of hot *paella*, which had to be cooked in batches because the pots I was allowed to use were so small. In truth, if I had brought along my huge pans, the stovetop would not have produced sufficient heat to cook the large quantities, so the limits imposed by smaller pots made me work harder, but probably made the batches more consistent. Max had a few nervous moments: His lovely gray eyes were large as he passed through the kitchen watching me, but I didn't have time to understand how anxious I was. I watched saffron rice cook in three pots, then transferred it to a roasting pan to blend and keep warm in the oven, while I used one stovetop burner to steam shellfish over wine and bay leaves, another to fry sausage, and another to heat extra broth, trusting that I would be able to combine everything in somewhat sensible, tasty proportions. Max was not so sure about my timing, co-ordination, or the proportions. I needed his strength and extra hands to haul the hot, heavy Le Creuset pots from stovetop to the wall ovens, and to steady the pots so I could scoop and mix. I coaxed him along with quiet, intense directions as I focused on the various times and textures and Millie worked the crowd. She gave us timing cues during the cocktails, and moved back and forth, kitchen to living room, as she needed to blow off steam. Dinner happened— Max served the buffet, and every-thing did cook through; the rice was not crunchy! Second batch, third batch, and by then the quantities were more manageable, so Max's shoulders dropped, his eyes stopped bulging, and he began to relax.

"I thought we were in the shits on this one, Carol," he ob-served on a break in the kitchen, so quietly Sylvia couldn't hear him.

"We did okay, Max. This just needed us *both* to get it organized." Now I could smile. I trusted his steady presence. I counted on him for so many levels of support: He was my right hand when that was in a cast, my shopper when my left ankle was broken, my front-of-house manager for dozens of events, my aide-de-camp when I ran large crews, my prep person and all around lieutenant. Although I might be sweating in the kitchen, he presented calmly on the floor. Such a fine actor and dancer, arriving with grace and assurance on the other side of the swinging door! He was the only one who knew this was the first time I had made *paella* for thirty-five, and I could not have mixed everything in all the hot pots without him in heavy mitts to move and balance them all. It was the only time I made *paella* for a catered event, come to think of it. Afterward I thought of it as a culinary achievement for me, under the circumstances, and it was tasty. I just wish I knew the gentleman's history with it.

The Grand Dame was pleased with the party. Her dad was exhausted by the time *paella* was finished, so birthday cake was served quickly, and while the rest of the family lingered, we cleaned up in the kitchen under Sylvia's watchful eye. Nothing was going to disappear or be misplaced; she would see to that. I liked Sylvia, and she liked watching us work hard. I was careful to serve her a generous portion of the *paella*. She shared just enough family gossip, rolled her eyes at all the kids' incorrigible behaviors, and picked up the mop to finish the floor herself at the end of the evening. I gave her a hug and some cash, knowing her employer would not offer anything extra for the Sunday work, doubting the Grand Dame would even think of it. Actually, I had to remind the lovely lady to pay me the balance she owed, but I expected that.

JUST A FEW MONTHS LATER, the Grand Dame's daughter called me. This time it was to cater the *shiva* at her apartment on the Upper West Side, as Granddad had passed. I booked Millie again, and she stayed at the apartment long afternoons and evenings, all week, as I shuttled food over, supplementing the gifts brought by visitors, making sure there was coffee and cream, sliced fruit and freshly baked sweets, and small savory bites for the people who drifted in and out around the children, the husband, the ongoing household during this mourning period. I was sorry I hadn't gotten to learn the story behind the *paella*, and hoped Millie would.

She continued to work for this family for years afterward. When there was a large gathering, and her skilled hands would make things go more smoothly, she was asked to serve. She never did learn Granddad's story, but she heard plenty of other tales about the extended family, and she kept quiet on the floor.

Millie was the kind of panther-parent you would want on your side battling for kids' needs in New York City public schools. Adorable as a kitten, she had stunning verbal skills that only came forward when her talons were needed. She could slip into the shade at catered parties, taking care of the details no one remembered—and she made sure those details did not get to be a problem.

I don't know if her husband stayed with the family, or

drifted along his own path. I hope her girls grew to be as strong as their mother. I never watch daytime TV, so I don't know if she was able to continue acting. She may have found other work by now; she would survive.

Eating Dis/Order

S HE OPENED THE DOOR TO GREET ME, in leopard leotards, tipped forward on red mules, leaning toward me with half-inch lashes fluttering like wings. "Won't you come in? Pat says you are just terrific and I want you to cater my *very special* birthday party! It's going to be here, so let's talk here, in the living room, here where we can set up for my guests." *Did she think I wanted to talk in her boudoir? And how old is she admitting to be?*

"What a lovely, spacious room. You have a great view!" I said. This part was easy for me to appreciate. I looked out, past the animal-fur coverings on sofas and divans, through floor-to-ceiling windows offering an East River view hovering over the Fifty-ninth Street Bridge.

"I'm celebrating turning forty—can you imagine! And I've invited about twenty-five of my very best friends to dinner! What do you think we should have?"

I appreciated her directness, cutting right to business, but I doubted some of her facts. *Forty, really?* "Well, let's start with some of your favorite items." Taking a hint from the décor, I asked, "Do you like wild game? Tell me some *hors d'oeuvres* you like that I could serve your guests as they gather."

"Well, I was really hoping *you* would propose some menu ideas. . . ." She seemed a bit disoriented, as though asking for her preferences made her uncomfortable. I whipped out several pages of neatly typed, elegantly worded menus, that I never ever sold. Clients picked elements from them. People rearranged the mushrooms from one dish into another, and took great delight in their creative adjustments to my proposals. I was used to this customizing for clients, no problem.

"I don't like any of these."

Well! I took a breath and brightly tried to pick up the conversation again. "We're not limited to what's on a printed page! Here in New York, there's so much available in the market. Have you eaten out somewhere that you found memorable? Have you seen something in a store that looked appealing to you?" *Give me some crumb to go on, leopard-lady.*

"Well, do you know that chicken Meditteranee-e-e-e they have at Grace's Market? It's just downstairs, a couple of blocks—it looks *so* good!"

"Great! I haven't eaten it, but I can go by later and check it out. If that's appealing to you, I certainly can attempt to make it, or at least my rendition of it, for you, and we can put it together with. . .well, how about wild and basmati rice with shallots and buttered pecans, and perhaps a julienne of spring vegetables, what I find best in season now?" *I'm on a roll, we have eye contact, and she's listening to what I'm saying.* "Then, we can decide on a first course, a dessert, and *hors d'oeuvres* to build around the main course." *Do we have contact? I tipped my head, checking to see if I'd pitched the menu too fancy, too plain, what?*

"Well, maybe. But what would you do with veal, if I wanted veal?" I went around the taste charts in my brain, and we talked about chanterelle mushrooms, three different sauces, various vegetables. Then she asked about fish, beef, and pasta options before circling back to poultry. I kept up with her, feeling like a show horse taking the usual pattern of jumps around the ring. *No missteps, don't nick a fence, the judges are watching every move.*

Thirty-five minutes on main course, and then, after all, that first chicken menu seemed the one she most wanted. *Is she unsure of me,* I wondered, *or is this her anticipation of the conversation about prices?* We spoke for just a few minutes about *hors d'oeuvres.* It was easy for her to pick those off the printed sheets, after all. Once she had heard my whole performance, they didn't look so bad to her anymore.

Then she shouted, "I want the *richest, most delicious chocolate cake ever!*"

I could relate, I love dessert and it is important to finish a special meal with something great. "I make a flourless chocolate mousse cake—"

"*Yes!* Yes! Yes! Yes! It must be—oh, so rich, rich, *rich!*" There was no hesitation there; she was close to orgasmic.

"I appreciate how passionate you are about chocolate! I'll make you a rich chocolate cake, no problem!" *Finally, we had connected! Thinking of great chocolate, we were both grinning happily.*

"Okay, get back to me with the cost estimate, please. I have to go now." I was dismissed and ushered out after precisely fifty minutes. *Uh, oh.* I had a peculiar sense as I waited for the elevator.

Sure enough, someone got out and headed for her door as I entered the elevator. Either competitive bids for this party, or she was a therapist. I shuddered; catering for therapists had created some pretty odd experiences for me, but that's another story.

I called her the next day with prices. She dropped several of her extras and hired me—all very direct, not much dickering around. She had already put me through my paces, and it seemed I'd passed.

THE NIGHT OF THE PARTY, I warned my crew, on the drive over, not to be thrown by the animal furs. As they interrupted me with comments on the oddities they observed among people and animals as we drove past the Central Park Zoo, I described the décor, the view, and the hostess in the most neutral terms I could muster, but they all read between my lines.

"So, Carol, she's gonna greet us in her black see-through negligee, just to see if John flirts with her, right?"

Was this a dig at my stunning, blue-eyed bartender, or was this Bobby's fantasy about ladies who conduct meetings in mules?

"No, Bobby, she'll be in her birthday suit, and you'll have to keep refolding her napkin!" This from Lilia, my saucy "kitchen-wench," who was trying to get Bobby to quit his full-time gig and work with her at her daytime job representing graphic artists.

"You are just jealous, because even if you borrowed her four-inch mules, you still wouldn't be able to reach across the table!" Okay, so Lilia was short. Still, she worked hard and had pulled my kitchen through many tough events.

"But she does such a great job in the kitchen—keep her where she belongs." John was waltzing to the edge of sexism. "Where she can reach what *you* want most!" he teased, backing up to play off Bobby's obvious pleasure and pride in our food.

I was the only one with a mental map of the space we were going to work in, so in between the word play, I described the L-shaped kitchen, the logistical problems, how we would set up rented tables and chairs in the living room, and bring food in one door and bus the dishes out through the other end of the tight kitchen passageway.

A mature man opened the door for us. He had a kind smile and made it clear he was needed in the bedroom, as long as we were here and knew what we were supposed to do. I was happy to see he was clear about his mission; we had our own, and I preferred to stay focused on catering dinner and let him handle the hostess.

We kicked into gear as only people who know one another's strengths and weaknesses can. Everyone's hands were full; everybody moved utensils and foods into the kitchen, pulled rented tables into the living room, and set china and glassware out of harm's way. Lilia immediately made space in the refrigerator and on the counters, and set up a cutting board. Bobby and John together opened the legs of tables, set them upright and adjusted without scraping the floors, set out linens, and found the napkins. As John began to organize his bar, Bobby dressed the tables, adjusted centerpieces, and sat down before the pile of napkins, so John started in again. "Hey, Bobby what kind of a fold ya doing? Is this Napkin Folding 101?"

"No!" Lilia barked emphatically from the kitchen. With the swinging door propped open, she wouldn't miss an opportunity for a tease. "Bobby's Bird of Paradise variation is definitely Napkin Folding 300, graduate school!"

"Post-doc in napkins next, Bobby? Or would you like to just try bartending?"

John was one incredible bartender: He remembered guests' drinks throughout the party, and, even more amazing to me, he remembered hosts' drinks from one event to the next, even a year later. It sure wowed the Austrian Trade Commissioner to see us setting up for a second annual event and, before he got through the room to say hello to his lady, the bartender handed him his drink, with a slice, not a twist, just as he liked it. John had an astonishing memory for faces, drinks, quantities consumed, and party jokes.

"Oh, I think I'll just rotate into the kitchen next, John. I don't want to put you out of work. Your daughter needs to eat." The reference to eight-year-old Amelia silenced John for a fraction of a second. If you weren't watching for it, you wouldn't have noticed.

"Hey, do you know who's running this Saturday? I took Amelia with me last week, after school. We went out to Aqueduct—she had such a great time!"

"Did she win?"

"Yeah, yeah, she always wins. She's the good luck charm—er, Bobby, pass me that flat, will ya?"

"Sure, John. I know you don't like to lift as much as you like to haul." "Ass" wasn't uttered.

"Well, I do prefer the 'lift and separate,' but—"

"Hey, boys, *watch it!*" Lilia wouldn't let them get away with that old Playtex Living Bra ad, not for anything.

And I was ready to steer them toward a last-minute strategy session, so the banter had to end: I needed to project authority. "Ok, here's the menu. First course, salad, set out as the hostess calls them to the table. Bobby, we'll give her the signal when we have salads set and dressed. Both of you guys will sell them wines as they're seated, then bread them – Bobby?" I waited a second for his nod of acknowledgement. "Are the butters cut, Lilia?" She hopped to that task, one she usually didn't need to be reminded about. *Have all the animal furs upset her or has her boyfriend flaked out again? I'll ask as we set hors d'oeuvres.* "Let's butter them before we set salads, okay?"

"Why don't we bread them as well?" This, from efficient John.

"'Cause we're giving them choices, so I've got to ask you to show them the bread basket first. I hope you don't mind!" *Don't be snide, just hold authority.*

"Just takes longer, you know," a grumble, coming from too much banquet experience.

"The hostess requested a bread choice, so we'll give them a

choice. She's paying, and you're staying, so if they've got to wait for their next scotch, so it goes—hey?" *Not much challenge,* I note, *just a poke, how he would like to get it done, but not how I've sold the gig.* He's so capable, he could manage a huge establishment, not just tend and serve for me, but he's just finishing up college, just starting to define his goals, just starting to get himself out of debt, out of a marriage, out of his thirties. John had so much old business to clean up before he would really come into his own. He would do it the way I asked him to, though; I trusted him.

"John, you will probably need to freshen up the drinks. Lilia, we'll get the veg going as soon as the salad goes out, and pull the plates out of the toaster."

I was referring ironically to the oven, where she had already set them to warm. "We've got chix tonight, folks. They are sitting at five o'clock, the veg at 7:00, and the rice up top at noon. Please be sure the chives are upright, leaning toward 11:00 a.m., not dead on their feet! Lilia, want to give them another trim? All cut to four inches, so their butts are fresh? Thanks."

She moved silently from the butter to the chives, remembering to wipe the knife, the board, and her hands. *Seeing her steady now; I'm thinking it's her boyfriend.*

"Dessert is the flourless chocolate mousse cake. I'll whip the cream. Please remind me to tumble on the fresh razz— they're in the fridge. We'll do coffee and tea, then follow with the little ones." They'd all seen this menu pattern before, all knew about my signature petit fours, my "kiss" at the end of a dinner party, a surprise for the hostess and indulgence for the guests.

"I've got plenty for us to eat." No surprise for this crew. They've been through plenty of dinner parties with me. "Although with these kitchen openings, let's be discreet. We'll see how much attention they'll want as they munch. Maybe more wine and water once or twice, another bread round, Bobby, yeah?" He nodded, but he didn't need a review of this drill. He patiently tolerated my words as I reassured myself. He reached for a roll, John joined him, and Lilia picked at some veggies. I always fed my staff. I wanted them comfortable and sure of their tasks as we started into an event. Sometimes, meeting a client, I felt like the horse taking the hurdles, but when a party was about to start, I was definitely in the saddle, firm in my seat with strong hands on the reins. In that time before the event, I was working the bit to gather my crew's attention. I wanted everyone to have a last-minute review to focus, to giggle together about something, to find a bite to eat.

Sometimes dinner parties just broke so hard! Guests arrived, and everyone moved constantly for the next five hours. Staff would look up at the end of an evening and realize they had worked their day job, run to meet up with me for the evening gig, and not seen food or drink since lunchtime. By 11:00 p.m. they were ravenous and not in any mood to break down tables, rinse off plates, neatly pack away linens and cutlery, or do any extra favors. Things got broken and lost in those hours. I always thought it the better part of wisdom to bore them for a few minutes just before company arrived, offer them hors d'oeuvre samples, bread, veggies, and a promise of protein once we were through the rush of our service. But sometimes, there was no break, no chance to catch real food during a party. This L-shaped kitchen with its doors at both ends would make discreet nibbling tricky.

While they snacked, they set their own directions. In with the "dirties" this way, out with the food that way; John solved that problem and vied with Bobby for who would lead for the evening. They worked like dancers: the choreography was instinctive, internal, balanced. They could "read" the room, exchange imperceptible eye signals, and never duplicate one another's efforts. I mostly missed their sign language, but I sure relied on it. They didn't need me to urge them toward the evening's hurdles on the floor; I merely gave them their head and let them run the course. I had to get the dinners plated in time for speedy delivery. I could work by myself against three typical waiters, but these two guys were faster than that. I needed Lilia's hands in the kitchen to keep up if anything was ornate on a plate or I had planned too many elements. Get the plates up and move them out on cue, or I would bore these men and they wouldn't make time to work with me. I didn't want to lose them; their skills handling people on the floor were crucial to keep my business going.

Just as they figured out the plan for bussing the living room, the doorbell rang. "Company," I said unnecessarily as we each moved to our stations. Bobby went toward the door to see if the hostess wanted him to open it to take coats, John loosened soda bottle tops to be sure there would be no spills, Lilia checked the oven temperature and started to garnish hors d'oeuvres. I began to design the first tray to be served.

It was a busy party, no breaks straight through to dessert service. Lilia backed me up double-checking those chives and sending out perfectly matching plates, and then she received all the "dirties" on their way back in and got them rinsed and into their return crates, out of our way, with minimal noise. I had sautéed vegetables, served up the rice, finished the chicken breasts with eight pans rotating on the four-burner stove, then whipped up the cream, sliced the cakes into clean portions, remembered the raspberries, and sent them out the door. Finally, I stepped back against the wall while the guys began the coffee service.

That's when our hostess pushed through the swinging door and came stamping into the kitchen. With great flair, she threw her leopard shawl over her shoulder, past my face, just missing Lilia's head as she worked at the sink. The woman planted herself in the middle of the tiny kitchen space, so the guys immediately adjusted service to continue through the other door, avoiding her.

"How could you serve *that?*" she exclaimed. "It looks like trash! How can you call that a *rich chocolate cake?* I wanted a *rich* chocolate cake! How can you *humiliate* me like this? I told you I wanted a *rich* chocolate cake! This is *terrible*, it is *disgusting*, it is *not what I wanted at all!*"

On and on she went while John and Bobby cleared dessert and, from around the kitchen corner, out of her sight, flashed the guests' empty dishes at me. They served coffee and the petit fours, which ended her dinner party with *ooos* we could hear even with the direct door closed as the guys ferried everything around the back way. The water kept running. Lilia rinsed off the dessert dishes, speeding through the mess, her eyes lowered to the sink as I faced my client. Despite the empty plates the guys were bringing back into the kitchen, and the happy party-babble noises we could all hear above the running water, she was a very, very unhappy client.

"This was *not* the *rich* chocolate cake I had in mind! This was just not what I *wanted!* This cake is *awful.* It is *not* the *rich* chocolate cake you promised!" The more she repeated herself, the more agitated she was growing. Suddenly, she reached into her freezer and pulled out a frozen Weight Watcher's Thinny-Thin Chocolate Bar. She began sucking it, biting into it, swallowing icy chunks as she continued her tirade of disappointment with the dessert, which she had *not yet tasted.* She kept repeating, "It is just not *rich* enough!" I kept my eyes on her, struggled to listen but more frightened by what she was inhaling. She was whipping herself into a frenzy, swallowing chunks of an ice-pop, endangering herself, not quite two feet in front of me. I braced to grab her, ready for the Heimlich maneuver. Then, just as suddenly as she had started, she threw the ice-pop stick into the sink, spun on her stilettos, pushed back through the swinging door, and returned to her role as party girl.

I saw the empty plates of a successful dinner party. I heard a jovial crowd, and my staff signaled all was well in the living room, but I was shocked—for just a few surreal seconds. I had never seen anyone eat anything frozen quite that fast. I was embarrassed before my staff, but I realized the guests were unaware of what had happened.

A bit unnerved and exhausted as I drew toward the end of my eighteen-hour day, I asked the staff, "Was the cake off? Was something wrong out there?" My sincerity was the trigger for their meltdown; they all went hysterical, giggling as quietly as they could, rolling into one another, and sliding down the walls. They had each witnessed some of her behavior, both in the kitchen and in the living room. They each testified to the guests' pleasure and her surprising behavior. They had scarfed down crumbs from a miss-cut slice of the maligned cake: They *knew* it was good.

At the end of the evening, the kind gentleman who had let us in came over to thank me, pay me, and offer a generous gratuity to my staff. I was grateful to be dealing with him: He was rational, calm, content.

"It was a lovely evening," he said. "Thank you all so much. That cake—ah, it was luscious, rich, wonderful! And then everyone was so delighted with the petit fours—that was a real extra treat! We'll all have to diet tomorrow!"

As we loaded up my equipment, packed the rentals out of the way, finished the last-minute clean up, and moved to the elevators, I quietly asked him, "So what kind of work does our Birthday Girl do?"

He proudly answered, "She is a weight-control therapist!"

I kept my smile steady as I backed out the door. Of course.

Catering Stuff I Carried

KNIVES! A CHEF'S KNIFE, PARING KNIVES, a bread knife, cheese knives, butter knives. Cutting boards and wooden cheese boards.

Heavy-duty garbage bags and Zip-Lock bags in two sizes.

Aluminum foil and plastic wrap, baking paper and butcher's wrap.

Kosher salt and a pepper mill.

Hot mitts and trivets.

An ice scoop, kitchen tongs, slotted spoons, and salad-serving tools.

Plastic food-handling gloves, and heavy-duty rubber wash-up gloves.

Non-abrasive scrub pads and dish soap.

Safety pins, straight pins, and an emergency sewing kit. Extension cords, Sterno, and an extra light bulb.

Piping bags and tips.

Cheesecloth and string.

Floral tape and florist's frogs.

Ramekins, dip bowls, and glass bowls.

Serving trays and bussing trays.

Wine pulls and corkscrews, bottle openers and extra corks.

Coffee urn and tea filters.

Wooden spoons, serving spoons, and tiny knives and spoons for dips.

Side towels and lint-free dishtowels.

Plastic-backed paper tablecloths.

Aprons and bow ties for front of the house.

Aprons and an extra chef's coat for back of the house.

Doilies, and too many skewers and even more beverage napkins.

Toothpicks.

Butter.

Fresh herbs, lemons, and limes.

Amulets and Advil.

Band-Aids and burn ointment.

Cash.

And, sometimes, a hand-held blowtorch.

Working
Mom

1986–88

Holiday Roast Goose in October

WAS RECOMMENDED TO A PUBLIC RELATIONS agent by a colleague who knew I had years of solid experience catering corporate and social events in a variety of settings on limited budgets. I was accustomed to earning my profits and my reputation at each event, but this agent, Joan, made me think I *really* needed to screen clients more thoroughly.

She was representing Bahlsan, the German cookie manufacturer, seeking press coverage for holiday *stollen* and spice cookies to hit print media before the Christmas season, and so the event was scheduled to the imperatives of press deadlines, in late October 1986, long before social media and the internet broke through the time barriers for advertising placements.

At our first meeting, Joan, as my client, made it clear I was not to take advantage of her (she was a knowledgeable cook!) or her client (whom she would fiercely protect!). Since that was never my goal, I worked first to get her to tell me what she needed, define the event she was conjuring, and then we would discuss a fair price.

It was rare back then to find public relations professionals who knew how to start a wine reduction sauce or save a breaking Bearnaise, but when Joan wanted to show me she knew something about cooking, I listened politely. I had my own inner voice of reason sometimes, but that day it was at odds with my need to pay the rent after a slow summer: *Carol, she is a loon— get out of here.*

"Joan, I'm sure we'll be able to do a great job on this. It sounds like a fun idea!"

Carol, there is no way you are going to find Christmas decorations in October, and you have never eaten goose in your life, let alone cooked three! She has no idea how many people will attend. Why is she dictating the amount of food you are to provide if she doesn't even have a guest estimate? What is this? Get out now!

"You can serve small bites of goose, on bread slices, with all kinds of trimmings, with the Bahlsen products displayed to fill and decorate the table," Joan said.

Carol, that is not *going to* work: *Listen to yourself!*

The budget began tighter than tight, and as her guest count climbed, she demanded I stay within the budget parameters we initially agreed to. I was polite for weeks but cringed when the phone rang a few days before the event. Joan enjoyed her many inspirations. She enjoyed insisting upon irrelevant changes, and she waxed eloquent about dinners she had eaten, and events she had attended, in the last decade. I was okay for her first three calls in a day, but by the sixth I was close to becoming nasty.

Carol, I told you so.

A fourth call, two days before the event: "I think we should set the food out on the second floor. Then the Christmas tree will be at the foot of the stairs, and we can have displays on the third floor." The kitchen was on the third floor, and I was quite certain no one would climb the extra stairs to look at boxes of cookies lying around. The tree blocking the stairwell was a very bad idea as well, even if the fire department allowed it. Despite the problems of hauling everything up to the third floor and having wait staff pass trays coming down the crowded flights, I thought it would be just fine if I was up on the top floor and had a bit of quiet in the kitchen during the event. I'd not been feeling very well lately.

The fifth call that day: "Carol, I really want the food to be set up on the third floor. I think people won't go up to see our merchandise unless they are drawn there for the food. Okay?"

Okay, so I'd give up the quiet for the closer access of kitchen to food table, which initially I thought made more sense. Perhaps then we would have enough food: Really, who was going to climb two flights of stairs for a bite of goose?

Joan reversed her decisions in Calls #6, #7, #8 that day.

Carol, I told you so, but, no, you wanted to just suck it up and do the party! So, go ahead, see what it gets you!

I stopped answering the phone. I would figure it out when we showed up on location.

While Joan had checked out my credentials before committing to hire me, I'd neglected to check out hers. I should have fired her. I knew my business, I knew what information I needed in order to prepare and present the event she wanted, and too late I learned she was not willing to pay for the quantities needed for the event, which kept growing. I didn't like her enough to coach her through every decision multiple times or to hold her anxious hand for hours of telephone calls. I was not being paid enough for all that. She was what I later came to recognize as a high-maintenance client for whom I (later) created a surcharge, attempting to cover my own therapist's fees when such counseling services had to be rendered in the guise of catering.

Although our discussions began in August, Joan was tentative about her commitment to me, to decisions we made and remade, and she was reluctant to give me a deposit right into October, about two weeks before the event. I had to order specialty flowers, fresh cranberries, kumquats, and geese: I really had to have money in my bank account before I went shopping, booked staff, or plotted out my own working schedule.

I had asked a couple of staff to hold the date, but as Joan's commitment remained tentative, by those last two weeks my usual crew were all otherwise engaged. Each referred me to a friend or a friend of a friend, whom I hired based on their second-hand recommendations, a not-uncommon practice for cater-waiters at the time. But it meant all my staff for the event would be men I had never met before.

Joan finally hand-delivered her deposit check with a long discourse on her fabulous recipe for Mock Lemon Mousse, which she really wanted to tell me about in detail, but I'd put her off until after the event. I ran her check to the bank, hoping it would clear quickly.

I began my work. I placed my specialty orders, reserved three geese, and made chutney and relishes. I'd read about roasting geese but when I had purchased them from a fine meat house, I wondered how one timed and tenderized what looked like three deep-frozen cement blocks. They were days defrosting in the refrigerator, and I checked on their condition after each of Joan's calls. I spared Joan but stuck my head in the refrigerator and spewed my true commentary all over their unrelenting carcasses. By the time I was ready to roast them, the morning of the event, they still had not thawed; they were barely softer than wood. I left them soaking in a sink of warm water, still in their wrappers, as I ran out to pick up last minute items.

Those geese were as unyielding as my first mother-in-law, who often lounged around soaking in a warm bath and then embarked on her cruel vendettas. What would the geese do to me?

When I returned from the last-minute shopping, I stored away my purchases, figured out a relish to replace the unavailable fresh cranberries, and cranked up the oven. Then I undressed the geese, seasoned them, and told them their time had come. Feeling much like Hansel and Gretel's witch, I cackled at them, and in they went.

I was getting myself into the mood of the event, muttering all the Yiddish and bastardized German I knew as I moved on to other preparations. Half an hour later, as I opened the oven to check on the geese, their powerful aroma caught me off guard. I left the oven door ajar, ran into the bathroom, and puked.

That was just the first time. Each time I checked on the geese, I braced myself, but I lost it. They never did get tender, but they had to come out of the oven hours later when it was time to leave for the event. I judged them "as-done-as-they-would-be," packed up, tried hard not to notice the green tinge on my face in the mirror on my way out the door, and sent the dollies rolling. I needed my strength to face Joan, whose calls I had not answered at all that day, and I needed the mental clarity to get through the event, directing staff I had never met even as my stomach roiled and my head repeated: *Carol, you are a fool to be doing this. You should have quit on her months ago!*

The three young men were all on time and all intended to be helpful; they were handsome and loquacious. I thought they would be a fine crew, if they were skilled. Experience was just a bit lacking in two of the three: They each had worked about three prior events between auditions for spots on daytime TV. On the drive over, I heard a lot about their auditions, and as we were unloading and hauling everything up to the third floor, and they were setting the dining room buffet table on the second floor, and setting up the bar on the first floor, and sorting out for service.

Carol, never hire unknowns like this again!

I set up the food on the second floor. I knew Joan wouldn't remember her last instructions to me. We, the caterers, had the third floor pretty much to ourselves. A good thing for me, as it turned out, but hard on the staff, crowded for the guests and chaotic for Bahlsen and the people managing the townhouse.

We were well under way when Joan arrived, bringing a wave of chaos with her. She wanted everything changed, it wouldn't work this way, the buffet had to be downstairs, the tree upstairs . . . . I squared off, planted my feet, and said, "No."

I turned my back on her and continued to set up in the most sensible fashion I could given the space constraints, everyone's changing expectations, and the onslaught of press arriving early. I was muttering to myself, or perhaps to the geese, while fighting to hold down my stomach. I called my staff together. I explained that I was not feeling very well, but that they had to listen to *me*—*I* was paying them, and they had to disregard this crazy lady or we would not survive the event.

"Whatever, boss." The two gorgeous men were gone emotionally, just waiting to be discovered.

Carol—idiots, you hired idiots!

But the third guy, who worked for a really serious chef, looked me in the eye and kicked into gear. "Shall we set the bar on the first floor, so guests can have a drink as they arrive? I think the food is beautiful on that table—it looks right in the dining room, where it belongs in this townhouse. Let me know when you want me to help take the geese out, what else you need to arrange. I'll take these guys to get the rooms set downstairs. . .and oh, by the way, I can handle characters. I've had experience with that!" He chuckled, and we exchanged looks; we both knew who he worked for. Bobby instantly became my Waiter-God.

Over the next ten minutes, he established himself as Director of Service *cum* Waiter-God: I heard him tell the two beauties to keep their endless commentary down to a minimum, to fan the beverage napkins and line up the bar glasses.

Then things got moving so fast, I didn't have much time to think beyond the immediate, necessary tasks at hand. Bobby and I began our duet, setting up cookie boxes on the buffet table; placing relishes, one goose, sliced breads and condiments; chuckling in the kitchen at some absurdity he had observed downstairs. Joan ran around rearranging everything. When she put her hands out to change the placement of the first goose, Bobby caught sight of my expression and quickly navigated her downstairs, away from my knives, urging her to address the imminent crisis he knew was starting at the bar, where one of my young men was trying to establish what drinks he was to offer. Joan had vetoed my suggestions of spiked cider or hot mulled wine, so there was a choice between white wine and water. Bobby insisted she was needed to participate in clarifying this for her unhappy client.

The other cater-waiter got his cardio-fitness program going that day, passing trays of hors d'oeuvres down the two flights from my third-floor sanctuary until it was time to help serve the goose. Then, under my tutelage, he learned to carve chips from the goose bones, bits of succulent flesh to be placed on slices of bread. But, as soon as I stepped away, he hacked the first one into massive chunks—the first six feeders at the event were obviously very hungry—and it was apparent the waiter lacked talent at carving.

Idiot!

I asked Bobby to swing over to that station. As if three geese would ever have accommodated a hundred and fifty guests!

Carol, why did you allow her to dictate how many geese you would have?

Of course I remembered those conversations with Joan. She had to have her way with the calculations: the food budget, planned for ninety, would of course suffice if the event grew. "We don't have to feed goose to *everyone!* No more than three geese will be necessary! I won't pay for more—don't try to rip off Bahlsen!"

When the geese lay in picked-over lumps on the buffet table, half an hour into the event, she came screaming up to the third floor seeking the fourth, the fifth birds—where were they? It was so many phone calls ago, she had forgotten her own dictum, or perhaps she was demonstrating her concern for her client, performing a dramatic, courtroom-worthy defense against this catering rip-off.

By the time she arrived on the third floor, though, the event was about over for me. I had done what I was contracted to do, even more, preparing chutneys and relishes, to make up for the missing fresh cranberries, which were not yet in season and not available anywhere in New York City. My head was whirling wildly, my stomach was dancing oddly, and I really needed to find the bathroom, unsure which way I was going to lose it.

Bobby arrived in the kitchen right on Joan's heels, before I indulged my urge to pick up my chef's knife. He guided Joan to safety and found some other decisions she could dither about and discuss.

Later, he directed my staff in the fine art of clean-up, poured me and my dirty equipment into the car service, climbed into the front seat, and told the driver the address back home. Perhaps I said good-bye to the other two service staff; I'm sure I paid them, because they went away.

Bobby must have put food into refrigerators, dirty platters into the sink, and he must have shut the door behind himself; I don't recall doing any of that. I was so grateful: I hadn't puked at the event, Bobby had been such caring help, the event was over, and I had my head on a pillow. I'd think about getting paid tomorrow.

When the telephone rang the next morning, I didn't answer, but I heard Joan raving, "Oh, it was such a lovely event! You'll get so much work from this!"

In all my years of catering, whenever anybody said that to me, it guaranteed I'd never get a single lead or job: It was the kiss of death. "Now, send me the bill and Bahlsen will pay you in a month or so. Thanks! Bye, bye!"

That was her message, but she had signed a contract with me just a few weeks earlier committing to make the final payment at the event. My little company was not going to carry her or the International Bahlsen Corporation for a month. I called her back.

"Joan, that was not our agreement. You promised to pay me the balance at the event. It was so busy yesterday, I didn't have a moment to ask you for the check. You agreed to pay me at the time of the event, and *you* would wait the month for Bahlsen to pay you! You need to get that check over to me *today*."

We bickered back and forth. Finally, I mentioned I had the business card of her contact person at Bahlsen, and I would let her client know about her double-dealing behavior. She closed the conversation saying she would bring the check over the next day, if she possibly could.

All kinds of face-saving went on in the next days, as Joan promised to come, cancelled, rescheduled, cancelled. Finally, almost a week later, she did come over, bringing her boyfriend as body guard. And she brought along a sample of the Mock Lemon Mousse. I tasted it but wasn't sure if she was mocking lemons or using Cool Whip in an unnatural manner. I still wasn't feeling quite myself, and through my spinning haze, I realized she was trying to sell me the rights to her perversion. And her boyfriend kept trying to renegotiate the amount he was supposed to write on the check.

I wasn't enjoying the exchange; I didn't like facing off against the two of them as I held onto the counter to keep my balance. I pulled out my copy of our contract, which she had signed without the boyfriend. I pointed to the balance, and to where it clearly stipulated the amount was due and payable at the event. I pointed, silently, to the amount again and again as their words swirled around the room. After an hour or so, I simply said, "Please, pay me, now. I am not going to buy your recipe, or anything else you want to sell me. Pay me, *now*." I could have puked—from him, from her, from the mock mousse.

Of course I never worked for her again or had any referrals from that event. I didn't know at the time, though Bobby later told me he suspected, that I would deliver an eight-pound, twelve-ounce boy the following June.

Bobby worked for me many years afterward—even babysitting in a pinch.

Election Night

REAGAN WON. THAT RUINED THE PARTY. But the guests had already been invited to take in the Fifth Avenue view, so the hostess figured, "What the hell, let's do a post-mortem." Conversations were completely on the blue side of the aisle, and the guests clearly felt they had missed some middle-American trends, those not visible from a Manhattan penthouse.

The hostess did not change her menu despite the election result surprises. We served an all-American chicken pot pie and salad, cookies, and brownies. She didn't know half her guests were vegetarians, or at least she didn't remember to tell the caterer. Vegetarianism was also a trend that I missed for several more years. Oh, humiliation! The caterer to run out of salad!

Bobby grabbed the lettuce off the cheese board in the living room as the crowd lined up for the buffet. With a quick rinse, he chopped, dressed and refilled the salad bowl, as I placed another chicken pot pie, hot from the oven, on the buffet. We squeaked by once Bobby got behind the line and measured out servings of the last of the leaves. There was plenty of pot pie and dessert.

It was Bobby's second event working for me. He was more loquacious and engaging with guests than I usually sought in staff, and although he was a few inches shorter than most of my tuxedo-clad male staff, guests seemed to respond to his warmth and humorous patter, his quips about Hollywood in the White House, better than I had anticipated. This change in service style, as well as the acceptance of women in service, was beginning to edge into catering, but I had not yet pushed clients hard for those changes, still grateful to be *myself* accepted as a female chef and business owner.

Bobby was so resourceful that night, he joined the ranks of Max and Thom as my newest A-Team Waiter God. Seems we all guessed wrong that year.

Fred Bridge Sold Me My Pots

OME OF US KNEW HIM as a grumpy but tender old bear. Others told tales of being thrown out of his store. Probably, those were the people who had asked for, and then ignored, Fred's advice. Bridge Kitchenware on East Fifty-second Street was the first stop for professionals setting up a commercial kitchen in New York City at the end of the twentieth century, and a favorite shop for serious home cooks. Fred's knowledge about quality kitchen equipment was legendary, and he only stocked the best. If you asked for his advice, you really ought to have taken it.

I had been into that revered shop over the years as I built my catering business. Now, well along in my pregnancy and about forty pounds above my normal weight, I went to buy pots for a complete new home kitchen. So much potential! So many gadgets, tools, and toys! What would I need for this new episode in my life: a non-commercial kitchen, in a house, with a kid?

As I gazed at the high-hanging collections, reading labels,

judging volume sizes, seeking home-cooking sizes, Fred bellowed from his perch on a stool across the shop, "Whaddaya wanna pay fer their advertising fer?" It took a while for me to realize he was addressing me: I was mentally slow at that stage of my pregnancy.

"Oh, I don't really, Fred. I just thought they were good pots." Such naïveté; but Fred had taken my measure. He'd seen me in his store before. He narrowed his eyes, studied me, and apparently decided he would try to educate me.

"Well, look at *that* stuff, over in the third aisle." This was his sales pitch.

I edged around the piles of boxes between the dusty, loaded ten-foot-high Metro Racks and into the darker aisle he had indicated, which was stacked well beyond my reach. When I was finally in the right location, Fred bellowed again, "Check those pots—triple layers in the base, copper-lined between double stainless layers, feel their weight, and *then* tell me if you wanna pay fer advertising!"

I had not asked for his advice, but it had been given. As soon as I lifted one sauté, I could feel the heft, the balance. It was obvious there was no skimping from this manufacturer to pay for ads, and there was no brand label visible either, which Fred knew. I looked around, unable to reach far without losing my balance, and realized I had to ask for help. That was a sacrilege in food service, the death knell of a woman's kitchen career in the 1980s, but the little guy was giving me a twist and kick just then. He was not so comfortable with all my reaching and stretching, and the protective instincts of impending motherhood won out. I backed out of the cramped aisle, waddled toward the cash register squared off protectively with counters and storage shelving surrounding the space Fred dominated, high astride his stool in the center, overlooking his domain.

Resting my bulk against his bulwark, I said, "Alright, Fred. Sell me the pots."

"Whaddaya need?" He was hedging, wary; did I actually intend to *listen* to him?

"Everything—an entire new kitchen, Fred. But a home kitchen. This isn't for catering." I had been cooking forty, eighty, three hundred, portions at a time. "What do I need for a home kitchen?" A home kitchen was foreign turf to me at that point. I had no idea how big my family would become. I had no idea of our plans for entertaining. I knew I was expecting a boy; didn't they eat a lot?

Fred looked at me silently, steadily. For a few moments I quaked; was I to be thrown out of the store for my utter ignorance?

"Well, if ya cook, ya'll want a good stock pot. And a generous sauté, a saucepan—two-quart, a double boiler is nice, butcha don't need it. Maybe get a lightweight one, just on occasion if you do any fancy baking. . . ?"

It was *kind of* a question, and I casually responded, "Not much."

He grinned. I had given the correct answer! I guess he didn't like fancy baking, despite the collection of jim-gigs displayed like altarpieces toward the back of the store. He went on listing what he thought I would need, and I stood before him, nodding compliance with his recommendations. When you stand before the master, listening is often the correct response.

Fred finished his list. I swallowed hard and sidled back to aisle three, wondering if my pregnancy-drained brain would retain half the items Fred had called out. I picked up the sauté I had inspected, slowly lugged it back out to the register. I went back down to aisle three again for the two-quart saucepan, gaining confidence in my recall. Fred bellowed again, but this time not at me, "Give 'er a hand! The stockpot, strainer, the big sauté's in the back!" He barked off his list again, rapid-fire. Lurking in the darker, dustier recesses of aisle six or seven stood another man, someone who helped find, move, and relocate the inventory. He was Fred's son. He slipped quietly forward, shy and not at all eager to engage with customers, but he carried out his father's commands. He packed my new pots into huge brown paper shopping bags, carefully swaddling them in extra bags. I handed over my credit card as Fred tallied up my purchases.

It was a significant bill. I had been a well-behaved and receptive, if somewhat slow-moving, customer. Five huge and heavy bags were lined up on either side of me. When I turned to thank him for his help, the young man had already faded into the back of the store. I sucked in my breath and made a deep *plié* in order to lower my arms sufficiently to reach all the bags while retaining my pregnant balance.

Fred watched. I gathered all the bags in my extended reach. I lifted them all. I didn't turn; I closed my eyes and crab-walked sideways, left-handed bags leading toward the door. I took one step, together, two steps, together. I was a chef. I could do this!

"*Stop!*" I knew he was bellowing at me this time. Surely, I was about to knock over some weighty, tilting display. "Put them down!" he commanded.

Slowly I *pliéd* to gingerly settle the bags back down. My belly didn't move: We were both listening attentively, still and waiting. From the dark end of the store emerged his son. Grinning broadly now, the young man hefted all the bags and urged me toward the door and a cab.

The pots are still perfect. Thirty years later, when I am asked the brand, I can still say, "I don't know, but Fred Bridge sold them to me." And I think of you, Fred, when my strapping, adult son grabs my heavy bundles, grins, and urges me to go on and open the door.

Applause from
The Manhattan Theatre Club

WHEN I WAS CALLED AS A SUBSCRIBER and asked for a donation, I whined that I couldn't afford to give more than the tickets I had already bought. Then I paused and asked, "But I have a small catering business. Would the theatre company want me to cater any events for them?"

That offer traveled quickly up the line in the development office, and by the end of the week, I had a miniscule budget to cater a party opening the next production. After that, it was a quick shuffle step to a very regular gig.

I read each script while the play was in rehearsal. I was given a very limited budget and free rein to create a menu that fit the theme of the show. I loved the plays, the young artistic staff, and the creative menu challenges. The Manhattan Theater Club was pleased to serve innovative, sometimes even exotic, menus on their box-wine-and-cheddar-cheese budget. At the time, no one thought to serve pierogies on a skewer, mixed with garlicky kielbasa, for the Polish play. My tiny cream currant scones and lemon curd tartlets were a sweet surprise at a British production, and the buttermilk biscuits with the slim slice of ham worked well (and were not messy!) for the Tennessee Williams revival.

This was how we worked in 1984, when MTC began to use the performance space on the lower level of City Center on East Fifty-fifth Street in Manhattan. It was an intense time of tight budgets and creative challenge, technical difficulties and a driving conviction that this theatre company had to grow. Barry Grove, the business manager at that time, and Lynn Meadows, the artistic director, wanted innovative champagne catering, but their limited funds went for the new lighting board, and they could not quite afford even a beer menu. So my New American Catering Corporation became part of the theatre family—we were insiders. I waived my profit, charged only to cover food, transportation costs, and staff wages, and began a long-term relationship between the Manhattan Theatre Club and New American Catering Corporation that justified my little company's placement right up there with the Fortune 500 sponsors in their playbill.

We used old props for our catering set-ups. We opened folded tables and set them in place, covered the blemishes with draperies and fabrics the MTC staff found. Flowers I had bought half-price that morning at the wholesale market became arrangements, tweaked and placed to catch the available spot lighting and hide their wilting blooms; baskets were up-ended to prop up other baskets, to fill visual voids, to position the inexpensive foods strategically for guest access and colorful impressions, with beverage napkins fanned out in neat arcs on front table corners.

My baskets and basic black trays served in multiple disguises, and no one got excited when something broke. Most of my staff worked both sides of the lights, and when they didn't have their own shows booked, they were happy to book catering performances for some steady income as we grew close to the theatre company staff.

We arrived just after the curtain rose at 8:05 p.m. to haul our food and serving equipment down the stairs into the temporary management office, and as the renovation projects shifted, we were shifted as well into the back dressing room. We set up food trays on any horizontal surfaces available for the night, trusting the Department of Health inspectors had already gone home, and we plotted lobby traffic flow while the audience watched the first act. We were totally out of sight during the intermission, but when the second curtain went up, my SWAT team swung into action. Half an hour later, when the house bartenders finally cleared out their stations and put away their cash and liquor, we pounced on the bar to line up steady plastic tumblers of the pinot grigio and chilled water our budget allowed.

We served six shows a year, Board of Director events, staged readings, fundraisers. We were hired upstairs as well, in the main entrance lobby, when City Center hosted fund-raisers for Twyla Tharp and other young, start-up companies. We were fast in and out, and we left everything clean and neat, as though hundreds of hungry hordes had not just passed through a National Historic Landmark. I thought it was supposed to be that way: That was how we worked in anyone's home, and it was our standard. Years later, I understood that our standard made my company special: It was not the way most companies actually operated at the time.

My fall seasons were marked by the invitational call from the MTC development office. It began as a proper *pas de deux* dance performance: The opening flourish and position held *en pointe* for the curtain rising. Then we swung into a standard, theatrical dress rehearsal: It featured overly dramatic expressions of mutual affection and careful discussions of how busy we all were; everyone marked their positions, blocked the scene from all perspectives.

Then came more practiced dialogue, to move the plot forward: "Would New American Catering Corporation still be able to support MTC this year?"

And then, my simple, but passionate affirmation, "Ah, yes!" and as the curtains rose, I leapt into their outstretched arms, our dance partnership renewed for another season.

I loved being part of that theater company. I got to know the administrators, the stage managers, the stars and all the lovely young women who worked in the Development Office. As they matured, one moved on to development work with Jacques D'Amboise and his National Dance Institute, taking me along to break and rescue hollandaise at his brownstone dinner parties. Another moved to Park Avenue and Seventy-ninth Street, where I appeared regularly in her kitchen as she attended to her husband's formal business entertainments. My connec-

tion with the Director of Development was a personal friendship that reached across the widest seasons of our private lives,
as our parents aged, siblings' marriages ended, and her young
sons outgrew bunk beds and the Little League.

In the fall of 1986, when I confirmed with my "Ah, yes," I
didn't know I was pregnant. I didn't realize for another three
months that pregnancy was bloating my belly, swirling my brain,
draining my memory, and altering my tastes for coffee, broccoli,
liver. . .*liver?* I couldn't say it! I downed Metamucil for weeks,
until my doctor insisted I take a break in my crazy schedule and
come in for an examination. Before I undressed, he looked at
me across his desk. "You're pregnant." The blood test proved
him right; he was an extraordinary diagnostician, and he knew
me well.

It was a bit shocking to realize, at thirty-something, that I
had missed my first trimester, but I was delighted with the
news. I began to figure out what I needed as I gathered baby information: my due date, diabetes test, sonogram, amniocente-
sis. My buddy Thom lent me his size 46 chef's jacket. The baby
was due on June 8, and my last booking with MTC was June 7.
I had never had a baby before but began immediate conversations with the "Meatpie," as we called my continuously ex-
panding girth, explaining to him that he couldn't come early. A
few months later, I booked an opening cocktail party for a bank
headquarters on June 18 and took time again to explain to the
creature now kicking in my belly that he couldn't arrive too *very*
late either (I was reading about kids needing parents to set
boundaries). But the MTC leaders, watching my burgeoning

belly, grew concerned about the timing for their last event.

"Don't worry, folks. The crew has been through this so many times, they'll do fine, even if I'm on my way to the hospital that night." The company managers were not totally ready to go with me on that; they wanted a back-up plan. Several of the young women from Development offered to understudy for me. They had watched our fun setting up in the dressing room, they adored the repartee with the handsome young men in tuxedos, and they loved the food. We all agreed we would play it by ear, improvise.

I kept talking respectfully to my Meatpie as he grew and grew, gathering a name, leg strength, and personality. I was sure we had an understanding. I felt just fine after those early months of flu-like symptoms.

Happily, although slowly, I shopped, prepped, and packed up that June 7 party, and we made it to the final curtain of the season: show over, lights up, joyful audience, good party-buzz. Afterward, we cleaned up, packed, and my crew hauled my equipment up the staircase as the MTC staff gathered in the lobby, now returned to its pristine state. I was always the last out the door, making one final sweep to look for the forgotten wine glass, the beverage napkin missed under a table, the last good-byes for the season. This evening, the executive producer, Barry Grove, took my hand. I thought he was about to lead me into a waltz, but instead he escorted me to the handicapped chair, attached to the rail on the staircase, and gently shoved my enlarged, unbalanced person into the chair and pushed the button. As the machine slowly lifted my hugeness up the stairwell, the entire MTC staff gathered in the lobby and gave me a standing ovation. I couldn't lean forward to bow much more than a nod, but the glory of that ovation still resounds for me.

My labor began the following day, and Will was born on June 10, 1987, right on cue and cooperating with the professional window I had allowed, just as we had discussed for the last several months.

Cherry Lane Theatre

HAD A DENTIST'S APPOINTMENT on Fourteenth Street, so I saddled up with the baby Snuggli, settled Will in with his legs straddling my chest, grabbed the diaper bag and my shoulder-strapped pocketbook, and boarded the bus for the ride downtown from the Upper West Side. I was taking my four-month-old out for a day's adventure. I was still nursing and didn't have baby-sitting arrangements organized yet but was about to learn I needed them.

Traffic was light, so we reached Union Square with an hour to spare, and it was overcast, so I didn't feel like introducing Will to the busy squirrels and drug dealers, chief occupants of the park in 1987. I headed up the stairs to Jack's Children's Shop rather than watch the street scene. I found a few little outfits for my fast-growing boy. I lingered over the barrettes and hair ribbons, buying too many for my nieces, but then, Christmas was coming.

I started down the double flight of stairs with the additional shopping bag and somehow I missed my footing. I was down on my back and sliding before anyone could help me. All I remember thinking was: *Keep the baby on top*.

By the time I came to a stop at the middle landing, Will was grinning up at me, showing his proclivity for fast downhill slides, which later emerged as a love of snowboarding. At that moment, all I knew was that he was safe, never mind my ungainly fall, the pain radiating from my left ankle, the heap of bundles and diapers and new clothing spread across the lower staircase. The little guy seemed to be wondering what my next moves might be as strangers helped me get back upright. Actually, they were all women, come to shop for their own kids and really happy *they* weren't the ones sprawled across that staircase. Someone offered to call an ambulance, but I was sure I'd never fit into anything smaller than an eighteen-wheeler with my bundles and swelling ankle. I had visions of some well-meaning EMT placing the baby on the sidewalk as they strapped me onto the stretcher and leaving him there as they packed me off to the hospital, so I said, "No, thanks. I'm on my way to the dentist. He'll help me out." I hobbled down the block, and the dentist was sympathetic but ankles were not his specialty, so he would not aim his x-ray machine at my ankle, and his staff was not going to share their private stash of ice. It was enough that one of them held Will while the dentist poked around in my mouth. He recommended I head to an emergency room for care, but really, just how did he think I would leave a four-month-old infant outside an x-ray room in a New York City ER? I understood that I needed a babysitter, asap.

I called my husband to meet my taxi outside his midtown office, on my way home, and asked him to bring a bag of ice for my ankle because—naturally—the icemaker in our fridge had recently broken. I continued home with Will, to nurse, change his diaper, turn on *Sesame Street*, and elevate my foot on the ice. I was beginning to suspect it was more than a "slight sprain," but there was nothing else I could do until Les came home from work. When he did, we three headed to the ER at St. Luke's Roosevelt Hospital. It was not a pretty place in those days. The x-ray confirmed a broken ankle, a resident practiced his casting skills, and around midnight Will was nestled in his crib, Les was rummaging through the fridge for some dinner, and I was back on our bed, seeking a comfortable angle to sleep with the new cast.

Since Will was safe and my ankle would heal, Les went to work the next morning. It took the second cup of coffee for me to realize what I was supposed to do that day, Tuesday, and all of what I needed to do for Thursday. I was booked to cater a surprise event for a young professionals group following a live stage performance. I was to set up a buffet with passed hors d'oeuvres for audience and performers. This was a new concept at the time: an attempt to engage young audiences in the arts coupled with a social "mixer." The show was *The Fantasticks!*, playing nearly forever at the Cherry Lane Theatre in Greenwich Village.

While Will nursed and I sipped my coffee, I thought about the staff I had booked for prep Wednesday and Thursday, for event service on Thursday evening, the shopping, chopping, and packing up equipment I needed to get done. Then I thought again about the shopping I needed to do for everything to begin to come together. How, exactly, did I think I could get myself through Fairway that day with the baby, the crutches, the yenta wagon—those four-wheeled carts doubling the sidewalk population? Shopping for seventy-five suddenly seemed daunting to me. It was early morning, but I called Max.

He got to my place at 9:00 a.m. I had to explain the detailed list to him: Cherry tomatoes, not quite ripe today—we need them firm to scoop out and stuff on Thursday; the German black bread squares; crème fraiche; and three pounds of smoked salmon ("Let them slice it for us, Max, while you gather the other items") for the canapés with dill garnish; the assortment of cheeses—in 1987 Morbier was a novelty cheese even for a sophisticated New York audience, and St. Andre was considered the height of luxury. We were a big step up from the cheddar-muenster–Jarlsberg served at large parties those days, thus demonstrating the sophistication of my client and engaging the "upscale" audience, even before we called them yuppies. I needed fine-quality white wine vinegar, more curry powder for the curried chicken salad, several herbs. I needed currants and a ripe pineapple to make my chutney that day, and I needed mushroom caps ("Just this size, Max, to stuff with spinach soufflé"—thank goodness I had that already made, waiting in the freezer!). I needed fruits to ripen for Thursday—melons, strawberries, another two pineapples not as ripe as the one for chutney, but not so hard it wouldn't be flavorful to use in two days. I needed smoked turkey and prosciutto, red leaf lettuce and two jars of honey mustard, a pound of fresh-ground chunky peanut butter for my crudité dip, and at least fifteen different veggies for the crudité baskets (so stylish then, thank you, Martha Stewart!).

The list was long. Max listened carefully, made notes, and rolled out with my cart around 11:00 a.m., just in time for me to nurse Will, change his diaper, and play with him a little as I confirmed staff for the event and scheduled the car service.

Max hauled back to the apartment around 1:00 p.m. with his ankles bruised, scraped, and bloodied by all the other yenta wagons that had rammed against him as he stretched long for the unblemished fruits far above the arms' reach of the old folks who made their daily trek to Fairway into their main activity and social center, colliding with everyone in the narrow aisles around the onion patch.

Max got everything and announced his executive decision to pick up the strawberries on Thursday morning, on his way over to finish prep. He could catch anything else I thought I needed then as well. I was impressed. He handed me the receipt, which reached to the floor, half his six-foot height, and proudly reported he had filled in the amount on my business check within sight of the food budget I had set. I was even more impressed. Then he collapsed on the sofa and bandaged his ankles while I unloaded the cart and several additional bags he had carried. I packed everything into two refrigerators and organized myself to start the prep while Will napped in the afternoon. Max had to leave for his afternoon rehearsal, so a sandwich, a kiss, and he was out the door.

I thought I was noisy as I clomped around on the kitchen

tiles, but it didn't seem to bother the baby. By the time Will woke up, I had two dollies lined up in the hall, milk crates interlocked and stacked full of trays, bev-naps, aprons, and service tools, topped with the lists of what else needed to be packed the next day, when I had staff reinforcements. I turned my attention to our family dinner and another hour of *Sesame Street*.

First thing Wednesday morning, Lilia and Bobby arrived, with Max right behind them. I had the coffee on and thought we would begin with a strategy session, but Bobby carried in the news: "Did you hear about the building collapse down on Commerce Street? I think it's on the same block as the Cherry Lane Theatre."

"Oh," said Lilia, "so *that's* why it was all blocked off. I had to go all the way around to Hudson Street to get to the subway this morning." Then she realized what she had seen. "Oh, will the *event* go on? Is the whole block in danger?"

I called my client to ask about that, and we spoke several times Wednesday, updated on the status of the Building Department inspection, the Fire Department investigation, and the Police Department barricades. In the kitchen, we listened to the local news reports as we prepped, relieved by the 6:00 p.m. announcement that Barrow Street was now open; the collapse on Commerce Street didn't seem to have compromised the stability of the nearby buildings, which mostly dated back to the eighteenth and nineteenth centuries. The party was *on!* Les would be home to take care of Will by 4:00 on Thursday.

However, when we showed up on Thursday evening, the police barricade had not yet been removed. The car service had to drop us off about a hundred yards from the theater. That's not an easy distance to caravan dollies, direct staff, and hand-carry baskets and pre-set trays of food and pastries—on crutches. At least Lilia's nearby fourth-floor walk-up apartment offered us refrigeration space for the pastries until after intermission.

Waving the food under the noses of the police got us past their barriers, and some extra cash kept the staff cheerful despite feeling we were walking through a war zone with building collapses possible at any moment, and all that rubble on the street! The police liked the pretty little tomatoes with dill feathers on top, the chocolate-dipped strawberries, finger sandwiches, and tiny cookies. We always fed the cops. We shared enough treats that night to get the blockades opened for us to walk through as we shuttled back and forth from the impatient car service to the theater entrance. I brought up the rear, fearing something might be left behind in the rented car service, tipping rather generously to contain the driver's temper.

We staged from the stairwell of the theatre, stationed between the second and third floors, to surprise the audience. We worked from above the theatre entrance and were required to allow the upstairs tenants to pass on their way home. Then, following the final curtain, the full buffet and trays of treats were in place to greet the hungry audience, who had mostly come straight from their corporate jobs, and the starving actors, whose hungers were deeply felt by my catering staff.

I had eight staff, but there were a lot of steps to travel, carefully. Lilia took someone to her home to retrieve the pastries during the second act. Working in the stairwell, the other crew seemed slow-fingered: We were not assembling trays as fast as we could with a set-up table. But the building remained standing, the food was good, and the audience was pleasantly surprised. By the end of the evening, I had broken through the heel of my cast and forgotten where I'd stashed the crutches.

Max helped me back to the kitchen. He made sure the dirties were all washed up and left-overs were put away in the fridge, while I supervised with my throbbing leg in the air, sixteen hours after we'd begun that day's work. I was hired for some sweet jobs after that sweaty evening, because this client knew I would take care of business no matter what.

My ankle has never been the same; I don't wear heels, ever, but I found a babysitter, "RaRa," the next week, at Fairway.

NARAL

N ARAL THOUGHT THEY COULD DO IT with volunteers, but the fight to support women's right to choose was harder than that; so was catering an event for hundreds of contributors. The leaders tried to keep the issue before the public—their image positive, their budget tight, and their fundraising effective. They understood fund-raising with a silent auction required food and beverages for supporters to remain in a generous mood with open checkbooks. I volunteered to assist with food service for the auctions for several years as my statement of support for women's right to choose.

Some of those years were a lot of fun. Great people poured into the kitchen from many different lives, offering eager hands and upbeat spirits. They were ready to prepare foods, serve the guests, and make a wonderful evening into a lucrative event for a cause they believed in. I had friends among the NARAL office staff, and they usually made sure I was assigned really involved, enthusiastic volunteers. One night, we set up a cocktail party in an art gallery, and I afterward hired those women for paid catering jobs. What a great source for new hires!

Some years, I was left in kitchens with ladies whose finger-nails meant more to them than the fund-raising goals of the evening. One of my friends had changed jobs, but others in the office asked me to run the kitchen that year at the Anti-Defa-mation League. Getting my kitchen knives through security took longer than the event was scheduled to run. The pace at which my volunteers sliced a dozen loaves of French bread meant that any other tasks I assigned would have had to wait for the next century. That was the year I learned how fast I could cut up roasted chickens and refill a buffet solo. I enjoyed watch-ing the activity among the bidders, laughed at the range of skills provided by the volunteers, and some kind folks came around to help with cleanup at the end of that evening.

The year after that, we were located at Temple Rodeph Sha-lom on the Upper West Side of New York City. It's a huge syn-agogue with a tremendous kitchen and generous gathering room for us to set up the buffet and auction downstairs from the sanctuary. The temple staff didn't hassle me coming in, but none could possibly be free to help me haul in the flowers, bas-kets, coffee urns, and foodstuffs I brought, until I flashed some twenty-dollar bills.

After 6:00 p.m. I had a few good volunteers, although they ar-rived a bit late after they had left their office jobs. Still, there were cheerful smiles as they donned my supply of black bistro aprons. They washed their hands, filled my coffee urns, nestled the white wine into my big buckets when the ice was delivered, and we got underway about a minute before the swarm of guests arrived.

The NARAL leaders greeted guests as they paid their entrance fees, volunteers offered a glass of wine, and people attacked the cheese boards before they began to browse the items up for auction. With a few moments to spare before the dinner buffet was absolutely needed, I had helping hands in the kitchen to bring out the platters of pasta, poultry, salad, and bread. Nothing was ornate, just good, fresh, and easy to handle to create a congenial mood for a relaxed, sociable evening, to encourage bidding that would cover event costs and generate operating revenue for the office to continue its work.

It felt good to me to use my equipment and contribute my services; it was my choice to have NARAL buy the food and flowers, and pay my staff to prepare it and my car service to deliver me. They would provide the volunteers to serve the event too, thus saving a major staffing cost and catering fees. I bore the extra pressure without my steady staff on location and with limited workers' hours to assist at the event, but I knew the volunteers were well-intentioned; everyone was making a contribution to keep the event running smoothly. There was just a bit of the thrill of the chase about that night, but we all pulled together and actually enjoyed some *esprit de corps*.

The following year, the office staff had completely turned over. Someone new answered the telephone each call in the weeks before the auction. I checked in several times to verify that I was still expected to organize the catering, to confirm the budget allocated for purchasing and preparing the food and be sure volunteers were being assigned to help me at the event.

Yes, yes, I was told, all was in order, just do what you've been doing these past years, yes, yes.

We were again at Temple Rodeph Shalom on West Eighty-third Street. When I pulled up in the car service, I saw some familiar faces, staff of the Temple, so I waved the familiar bills, and everything was removed from the car, set out on the sidewalk, then conveyed safely downstairs around 4:00 p.m. Plenty of time, I thought, for the volunteers to arrive and lend a hand. I started in on my first tasks: to get the cheese boards ready, the crudité baskets, the bowls and boards and bread baskets set at work stations for the volunteers to set up when they came. I asked the house staff to open a few tables and set the cases of wine and soft drinks where I was placing the bar, when the ice was delivered. The tablecloths, wine openers, beverage napkins, and ice tongs would all be ready as soon as the volunteers arrived. I pulled several tables into lines for the buffet and tossed tablecloths, to unwrap, on top, so the volunteers could cover them before the foods, baskets and flowers would be set out.

I stopped to greet the office staff when they arrived to open the guest registration around 5:00 p.m., expecting people to get there at 6:00, but when I asked about my kitchen volunteers, I noticed the palpable change in attitude with this new staff: They were angry, surly, and seemed quite miserable. And no one knew anything about volunteer assignments.

Back in the kitchen I began to open my armloads of flowers to decorate the buffet tables myself. At 5:45, I still had no kitchen volunteers, no tablecloths had been opened to cover tables, and no volunteer bartender was in sight. At that moment, my babysitter, Radhica (*aka* RaRa), arrived with Will. The plan I had discussed with office staff for several weeks was for me to set everything up, then flip the kitchen work to the volunteers during the event, take Will home, where my husband would put him to bed and I would come back for my equipment at 9:00 p.m. Radhica took one look at the situation, let William out of his stroller, and began to open the tablecloths. Will, not quite three years old, gathered the ferns and brought them out to the tables to help me decorate. I opened two bottles of wine to start the bar, brought out the cheese boards, crackers, and crudités I had already set up, then headed back into the kitchen to try to plate up some foods for the buffet—the hell with the flowers. Radhica filled the coffee urns, set up the plates and cutlery, and then, with a look of real sorrow for me, had to leave, now late for her evening job. As guests were gathering, Will politely took himself around the room to view the items up for auction: I think the early guests were encouraging him to buy something. His marks appeared on several clipboard sheets, so he was distracted for a few more minutes roaming that cavernous space while I kicked his stroller out of the way and hauled out foods as fast as I could to give some feeling of order and preparedness, which clearly was not the tone of that year's event.

I had asked for volunteers about four times before 6:00 p.m.; at 6:15, I screamed for them. Two dispirited, foot-dragging young people came into the kitchen with no interest in the tasks at hand and a seeming determination to appear incapable. They asked too many questions and stood in the middle of the kitchen, so I could not move past them. Obvious tasks overwhelmed them: "Please slice the breads. There they are on the counter, on the cutting board. The knife is next to the cutting board. Bring the filled basket out to the buffet."

"Please, bring out that platter of chicken—it's ready, and people are waiting."

"Please dress the salad—no, not the whole gallon of dressing on one bowl! Do you see the pans and pans of greens for refills? Perhaps a pint of dressing would be enough, don't you think?"

My frustration with their lack of sense, lack of good will, and lack of cooperation compounded as I tried to keep the swell of guests fed, moving along the buffet and out into the auction for the real purpose of the evening.

Well after the auction closed and the office staff left with checks, receipts, and their paperwork, my husband had to come for Will to get my toddler home to bed. No one helped me wash or pack away anything. I was there very late that night, and I got home in a really bad mood. Pulling together food for three hundred by myself was not the spirit of community, and not my idea of contributing to the cause.

The next day I quit NARAL. I suppose the office politics were no better or worse than those that rule in any organization, and staff change is inevitable, but I didn't want to cater a large event solo ever again. For that organization, too much was beyond my control as caterer. Another generation had taken over, thinking it would be so simple to change attitudes about women's right to choose, the volunteers could do it all. So I left it to them to figure out how.

Call the Caterer

YOU DON'T KNOW ME. I got your name from my friend, Irene Sax. She said you would be the right person to call for this." With a recommendation from a friend in the food press, she had my attention.

"I hope so. How may I help you?"

"Well. . .yesterday, my daughter Juliana. . .died. We have a service the day after tomorrow, and then her friends and some family will be coming back here to our house, apartment. Actually, I don't know how many people will be coming back here. What do you serve?"

I was stunned by the mother's nightmare. I looked over at my infant son, fought my own tears, then tried to keep the conversation moving, to gather necessary facts, get past the prestigious referral and hone in on the client's needs.

"I'm so sorry to hear of your loss. Irene is a fine food journalist. I'll do my best to provide what you need. Tell me, what time do you expect people?" I thought that was an easy question.

"Oh, I hadn't thought about that." She paused. I could hear her breaths. "We have the service at 10:00. A number of her friends wanted to speak. I think it will be over around 11:00." I added another hour in my mind.

"Will people be coming back to the house directly? Walking, or with cars to park?" Too rapid-fire—I stopped myself. Let her collect her thoughts. Let her tell you what she needs.

"Well, I don't know if they'll have cars. Many of the young people will be walking. Perhaps Juliana's brother will have his car. We'll be in a car. I don't know. . . ." As her voice trailed off, I understood she'd lost concentration and perhaps was beginning to grieve right there on the phone with me.

She pulled herself back. "Where were we? Oh, let's not worry about the cars. I just think they'll get to the house around 11:30. Is that all right? Can you be ready for them then?"

"Yes, of course I'll be ready. I'll set out some cold beverages as guests come in. Would you like a buffet set out, foods to be passed around?" I had no clue what she expected: What did she need to feed who-knows-how-many people come to mourn her daughter? How old *was* her daughter? She herself sounded fiftyish. Were we talking about lunch the day she was burying a young adult daughter?

"Well, I have a dining room table. It would be nice to have some foods there. Yes, some cold drinks when they first arrive. It would be nice to pass some little canapés. Wine would be nice. Cold white wine—Juliana liked that. Maybe coffee for later on? I don't know how long people stay. Do people drink coffee in the afternoon?"

Ah, there were clues. "That's fine, I can have a buffet with some traditional items: hard-boiled eggs, challah, a circular cake when people arrive. My staff will serve cold drinks and pass some hors d'oeuvres around as well." I wanted to know if there was a side table to set up for drinks, but I couldn't ask. I just made a note to bring extra plastic under-cloths to protect her furniture.

"I'll brew decaf coffee, so no one will be disturbed by caffeine, and we can set that up for a little later on, say 12:00?" Could I ask what food she wanted served?

"Okay." She sounded mellow then. Perhaps sedation was kicking in; perhaps, having made contact with me, she was over some hurdle. "Irene says you'll know what to do." I understood they needed some rituals respected, but her decision-making capacity was close to done. Still, I had to ask, "Could I trouble you for the address? Can you leave a key to your apartment with a doorman?"

"Oh, yes," she chuckled. "I really am not thinking so clearly just now."

"That's certainly understandable. I will have fine, mature staff with me. I'll bring all the equipment and a big coffee urn, to set up." I hoped my voice was reassuring her—if I filled in these blanks, later, if she thought about details, she'd know I had them covered. Would that help? Was this what a bereaved mother wanted to hear? I'd figure the rest out. I'd have to: I'm the caterer.

"Yes, yes, that's fine. Irene said you knew what to do—that's fine."

My reference made a sales pitch redundant, but there was some information I thought vital but wouldn't get. How many staff did I need? How many guests would be squeezed into her apartment? How much could I prepare for the day after tomorrow? What else was I supposed to do, in my life, tomorrow and the day after?

One more try—I'd have to go for it: "I need just a bit of guidance to develop a menu you would like. Can you tell me what foods. . .your daughter liked?"

First, that drew a stony silence, then tears, then, "Juliana liked salmon and sushi, light foods, healthy foods. She was in the theatre and conscious of her weight. All her friends are so attractive. She died of a brain hemorrhage—they couldn't do anything for her. Oh, but I hope this won't be too expensive! We really aren't wealthy people."

"No, I'll work with a modest budget," I said. "I'll have everything in order, set to go when you get back to your house. Don't worry about anything on my end. I do know what's needed." From the moment I hung up the phone, I scrambled for staff, cobbled together a menu, packed the coffee urn, gathered paper goods, scratched out the shopping lists, and rearranged my schedule.

I'd never met Juliana and I never worked for her family again, but I remember the afternoon sunlight striking the soda bottles on the credenza next to the dining room table as I arranged the fronds of dill on smoked salmon canapés in the small, bright white kitchen, as I handed staff more tissues to offer the guests, as we replenished the trays, as I sliced the ring of the fragrant sour cream Bundt cake I had baked that morning, commemorating the circle of life.

I remember too many details of young Juliana's *shiva*, as my son marches into his third decade these days.

Issues Beyond
The Food

1988-99

Thom Smyth Catering at MOMA

B Y THE TIME CAROL BOOKED the Weight Watchers Twentieth Anniversary at the Museum of Modern Art, I had
worked on and off with her for about five years. We'd
met when she was still the Director at the New York Restaurant
School. She had interviewed me when I applied but left before
I enrolled. When I got out and began cooking for Martin Scor-
sese, the student grapevine carried word she was cooking for Al
Pacino. I looked her up and asked if she wanted to work together. Sometimes it was her catering gig, and she hired me as
"Food and Design," and sometimes it was my gig, and I hired her
and the "New American Catering" crew. We both worked front
and back of the house; we cooked, set up food and floral buffets,
and decorated thousands of hors d'oeuvres trays.

For the MOMA event in the fall of 1989, she pulled in crew
from another catering company, doubling the insurance policies
and hiring friends who were friends of friends: anyone who was
well enough, had a tuxedo, and was available for the evening to

staff front and back of the house.

Bill helped me design the twisted wood, fabric, and textiles, and he helped me pack all the pieces into the Jeep. I stoked the fire, tucked the blankets around him on the La-Z-Boy, and left him with a hacking cough to face the lonely evening in the big old house. I drove down through the windy afternoon, orange and yellow leaves swirling around the hills of Connecticut into New York City dusk, reached the loading dock of the museum.

I was almost on time. Carol's vans were already emptied and off to the side. She spotted me, flashed a half-smile, and went right on directing dozens of staff I had never seen before. They were not a coherent team, and everyone needed instructions two, maybe three, times. Carol held a clipboard against her gray silk pantsuit, stumbled back and forth in her heels, and checked off too many details on her timed schedule, trying to set up tables according to the diagrams she had drawn.

Okay, I am here, I told myself. I turned off the motor and got out of my Jeep.

"Hi, Thom! Let's move on display immediately!" She sent two guys, already dressed in tuxedoes, over to help me.

"Hi, fellas. Would you grab those leafy, twisted branches over there? They need to land on the semi-curved tables, which should be dressed. It's a thirty-foot serpentine. Is that ready?" No, it wasn't, so they dropped the lumpy branches, fanned out the green tablecloths, and started to clip on the table skirts. Then I began.

I needed to get oriented. I shifted the tables' direction, under the massive hanging Calder, to understand how the lighting hit the tables. The branches and gold-threaded fabric swaths lay around the floor. There were too many tuxedoes chatting and muttering and shuffling by around me. Mentally, I willed them to stay at a distance. I cleared my head space.

The guards stayed close to everyone on the catering crew, certain we were all such assholes we didn't understand what was surrounding us on the walls. The museum staff hovered, insisting dollies needed extra-soft wide rubber wheels if they were to be used on the polished marble floors, and ours were just not good enough, so everything had to be hand carried. Nothing could lean against the walls; everything had to rest on movers' blankets.

Carol dealt with them. Tuxedoes kept swirling around everywhere, moving the rented tables, linens, and serving trays, moving the lugs of bar glasses to the left and then back to the right, and then back again. Carol dealt with them.

Dell was pulling out of the chaos in his kitchen just off the loading dock. The kitchen staff opened the cheeses, found the boards, unpacked the tools and bowls and display trays. Katy was not gaining command in the second kitchen; anxiety built with her repeated questions. Carol had packed more than they all needed. She had the menu covered, with back-ups and extras of everything possible should any item be lost or arrive broken. That kitchen was overwhelmed, but I had to let those images go; eventually they would figure it out.

I faced what I had packed with Bill. In the moment:

I find my breath.

I lift a section of tree limbs.

I shift the limbs slowly, set and change my angles.
I get the pieces in place, then
I shift them again, adjust.
I sigh. I must move on.
But it's not perfect.

I draped the shimmering fabrics, twisting them to catch what light was available. I set the smaller branches when I saw the larger structure emerge. Carol ignored my vibe, my need for more time; she came in close to my side to shift these pieces with me into places only I had seen, with Bill, somewhere else.

Suddenly, Dell sent out tuxedoes carrying six cheese boards and a dozen baskets of beautifully fanned crackers, but one tuxedo spilled a basket, leaned down to pick up the broken pieces, and began to spill another. Three more tuxedoes were carrying a tidal wave of fruit and nuts. "Wait! *Stop!*" Dell had jumped the gun, had not waited for Carol's signal; his timing was off. Carol dealt with them.

"Thom, company's here!" Carol's words were whispered near my ear as she caught sight of her employers approaching. I felt her shudder; barely holding a surface calm, she marched toward them to head them off. I focused only on getting it done, *now*. Carol dealt with them, then came back to me.

Katy emerged from her station, hissing, "There's no way to cook the chicken! The kitchen staff locked the burners!" The day crew had locked the burners at the end of their shift: a simple security procedure at a museum full of Picasso, Matisse, Cezanne, and de Kooning. Perhaps no one had told them caterers were coming in for the evening; perhaps they had been told and locked up anyway. I chuckled.

Katy's kitchen crew spilled out into the museum lobby to see what was going on and grab a drink off the service bars. The hosts spotted the out-of-place cooks and scowled at Carol. Confusion grew contagious. Carol stared into Katy's eyes and only I could hear her murmur, "Gather your crew. Set up just the cold items." Katy herded her staff back out of sight, back on task. Until that morning, Michael was going to run that kitchen, but he was in the hospital that night, maybe for the last time. Carol had asked Katy to cover at the last moment as best she could.

This event was all on Carol, and her heart was at the hospital.

I thought of something, though. "There's another kitchen upstairs, Carol. I can cook the chicken satay up there."

"Thom." She exhaled a thankful breath and was focused again, even as the tears slipped down behind her glasses and glistened on her cheeks. I stepped back from the tables, and then she received Dell's trays and baskets to finish shaping the tumbling masses of tastes and textures, edible disorder flowing casually over the structure. As the tuxedoes passed the trays to her, I grabbed their two sets of empty hands, and we went over to Katy's kitchen to take the raw chicken upstairs to the corporate dining kitchen. There, I grilled marinated skewers of satay for an hour, and the tuxedoes relayed them down to the party without spilling the peanut curry sauce.

I was okay cooking alone in the quiet kitchen. Carol worked the floor of that celebration for six hundred starving Weight Watchers. I stood there in Michael's place, backing up Katy. Dell would soon go back home to Kentucky, too sick to work anymore. Bill would not see our daffodils that year. I did the work that was needed that night. The display was not perfect, but we held it together.

Tequila Christmas

I WAS HIRED BY A SMALL LEGAL printing company to cater their 1989 Christmas party. They rented a loft in a warehouse building on West Thirty-second Street, a space used for fashion shoots, far from the madding crowd. It was near Dyer Avenue, a major north–south commercial road in the early twentieth century, then an entrance to the Lincoln Tunnel to New Jersey. Not much good was happening on the streets after dark with the truckers gone; the models were slinking around further downtown by then. The street could have been the set for one of those really grey scenes in *Midnight Cowboy*.

There was a tight limit to the budget that year. While the company had practically been printing money during the prior decade, it was a lean year, so the graphics team had been asked to "volunteer" to decorate the loft.

They asked me for a simple buffet and a full bar, and to go light on the service staff. The party was being planned for about 125 people, so I brought two bartenders and three servers to work the floor. I would handle the kitchen alone, with the food all prepped ahead, so it could be an easy night. It was a straight-forward event—no frills, not even a DJ, just the ritual of gathering to end the year and wish for better business in the new decade. The boss's wife didn't come, and my crew joked about her distaste for slumming in that part of town with such unsavory characters out and about, especially the catering staff at the eighth-floor event.

But the boss was a genuine party-guy, always ready to raise a glass, start the dance, and strike up a conversation with someone he didn't usually see in the office. His loyal staff came out for the party to bring some closure to the year and sign on for another, with "big changes" in company policy and directions, as he told it year after year. He was a big man with a big heart and the life-spirit that motivated the whole company.

But Billy, the head graphics designer, resented his extra-duty assignment. He couldn't get into the spirit of the holiday, and I was told he had really been riding for a fall the whole month before. He arrived at the space after we did, with a box of ribbons, balloons, and a helium tank but no other decorations prepared. He was stoned. The helium tank didn't work. He ran around shrieking for help, but he was unable to focus long enough to explain to anyone how to help him. Two graphics staff showed up, but they didn't know what he wanted, and they sure didn't know what to do on their own. Everyone sat around waiting for Billy to give them a task, discussing whether he would get himself canned that evening.

He grew more and more morose as we set up the catering.

Finally, one of my guys just climbed up on a bare table, took charge of the bits of decoration available, and aimed spotlights on the bar and near the food, trying to bring a bit of holiday cheer to the surface. I wanted to prevent people from tripping into each other, falling over tables and unlit chairs, so another staff member joined in support.

By party time, the room was still dark, but with color tints on the spotlights, we had created some sense of a mood in this otherwise forbidding space. White linens on café tables, and white plastic chairs, helped to define perimeters of the useable space. The food was set and the bar was organized, so I wasn't worried about my tasks, but I was concerned about the *spirit* of the evening. Billy was vacillating between gloom and verbose hysteria, blathering about his imminent dismissal for refusing to decorate the space.

I tried to console him. "Andy isn't going to fire you for this. He won't care, if everyone is having a good time. You'll see it won't matter to him. All year long you do your job. This was an extra. Relax, calm down, get a hold of yourself." Talking to someone stoned and frightened, it was not clear I had succeeded.

I had been catering for Andy and his company for years, and I didn't think Billy's offense would amount to much, especially if The Wife was not around to point out The Crime. The minimal decoration carried out the simple, pared-down tone of the party. I trusted that Andy would understand, and that the party would happen one way or another.

People began to drift in slowly, and about an hour into the

party, I left the kitchen and went over to the bar to check on the inventory and see what people were drinking. I noticed that about half a liter of tequila was gone and looked at the back bar, just to be sure we had a second one. "Who's drinking tequila tonight?" I asked.

Dave had not served any he could recall, but John said there had been one guy. "He's slight, blond, and curly, a bit hyper. He's the only one I think I served. Hey, I didn't *realize* half the bottle was gone!"

John immediately reached for the second bottle, pulled it off the back bar, and tucked it out of sight under the front table without me saying a word.

"That's Billy," I confided. "Please, cut him off if you have to. It's too early for this. He came here messed up."

I cruised the dark perimeter to see if I could spot him and to make sure the floor crew was keeping the space bussed, the mess contained. I did not want the surrounding darkness to be a pall on anyone's holiday spirit or offer temptations of a nefarious sort. I took the time to greet some of the company staff I knew, tried to joke and cheer things along.

Since the buffet was up, I had nothing to concern myself with in the kitchen, which was actually the model's dressing room, screened off with dark, plushy drapery, until it was time for the odious clean up. The water source was a slop sink, once we moved the floor mops and cleaning pails out of our way. I was glad the water had to boil in order to percolate the coffee through my urn and out the spout into human beings' drinking cups. I made a mental note to scrub the pots and percolate vinegar through them before I used them again. But I would not say anything about that to the company folks who had chosen the space: no need to point out issues that couldn't be addressed on the spot.

An hour later, I checked back at the bar. The tequila bottle on the front bar was in the same place, still half full. I asked John if the tequila drinker had switched beverages, and he looked quizzical for a moment. "Come to think of it, I haven't seen him here since you were by before."

I pulled back the table skirt to check for the secured second bottle, which was gone. "Okay, fellas," I said, "we've got a problem child." I went back onto the floor and grabbed one of my service crew. "We have a problem, Ken. Help me find him. Then I've got to ask you to do extra duty tonight."

We scoured the room and found Billy, head down on a table, in a very dark corner. Yeah, the tequila bottle was in front of him, and this one had about a third left in it.

I sighed. "Ken, this is Billy. Your job, and I mean the only thing I want you to do for the rest of tonight, is to keep him in view, actually within arm's reach. I want you to walk him to the bathroom and make sure he comes out in one piece. I want you to take him home in a cab. I want you to open his apartment door, get him in, and tuck him into his bed. I want you to lock his door behind him, and then I want you to call me, whatever time it is. Then you are done. Here's money for a cab—take yourself home in one afterward. As of now, you are earning double-time pay. Thanks."

Ken was a bit stunned. This was not the usual assignment

for a cater-waiter, but with double-time pay, he would not ask too many questions. We met eyes and I knew I could trust he would do the right thing. I headed back to the bar.

"Okay, who else is drinking heavy tonight?"

"No worries, Carol. Everyone else is going heavy, but under control. I guess it's been a rough year."

Well, yes, it had been, for many of us, and for many reasons. The economic downturn of the late 1980s had hurt lots of businesses and lots of relationships. AIDS was epidemic and growing wildly, wiping out many of the artistic communities of New York City and affecting lots of staff in food businesses. People were scared about their own behaviors, about other people's carelessness, and by the lack of real information. One big concern hitting food businesses revolved around fears that AIDS could be transmitted with the buffet plates. Caterers asked one another, "Does he look too sick to pass the hors d'oeuvres?" We mumbled about our fears of working for attorneys, as a general edginess in the city translated into increased threats of lawsuits, for services not rendered, for insufficient staff, for endangering guests. Insurance rates climbed for small businesses, if you could get insurance at all. If anything bad happened to Billy on his way home from the party, of course I would have been sued. So would my bartenders, the space where we were partying, the company, and the boss himself. There wouldn't be enough insurance to pay for all the lawsuits, but way beyond that, I could never have forgiven myself.

So I hunkered down that night and did Ken's part of the service. I paid him a lot to assure myself I had done all I could do to be certain that sweet, sad Billy got home safely, at least that night.

Billy was not fired, but AIDS caught up with him the following summer. He wasn't quite twenty-five, and he'd never had the time to learn to survive: to handle life crises, work problems, personal issues.

Ken is gone, too.

Anita

ANITA AND HER SISTER HAD BEEN abandoned by their father as teenagers, left to take care of one another and to watch their mother die of breast cancer. Years later, when I knew Anita, the sister had rooms for her cats in an apartment in Bay Ridge, Brooklyn. Anita visited and took care of the rescued animals according to specific instructions the sister gave her, but she never lived in Brooklyn again.

When I lived on the Upper West Side, Anita was my neighbor-who-worked-on-Wall Street. For many years, that was all I knew about her. I saw her at the elevator in the mornings. She wore clothes I admired—oh, my, that aubergine wool suit with the oxblood and ochre epaulet braiding! Her make-up was precise, her hair long, with huge larger-than-life brown curls full of highlights and invariably under control. Sophisticated products kept it all in place, maybe added another few inches. In winter, her dark silver trench coat shimmered, belted tightly and knotted just so.

Anita was petite too, maybe reaching five foot two in those heels, with a great, toothy smile and the skill with make-up to create her sparkle in the morning. Her large, dark brown eyes expressed open curiosity, intent behind oversized, windshield glasses. She had a warm laugh, but she reached for the laughter herself; she watched carefully to be sure you laughed with her.

She often had a quiet and interesting comment for me, and when I took my son to school, she offered that tremendous Julia Roberts smile for Will as I herded him into the elevator in my scruffy jeans. By the time Will started school, I was often on my way to Fairway after I dropped him off. Sometimes the three of us would walk together to the Seventy-second Street IRT Station and have a longer conversation until Anita turned into the subway heading downtown to her administrative work for a big hedge fund.

Her more outgoing roommate was Terry, an early-childhood teacher who had begun to work as a freelance curriculum writer when I was building my catering business. I watched Terry and Anita as we all aged through our twenties and thirties and into our forties. We all came from Brooklyn and we were old-fashioned neighbors: If I needed extra fridge space, they offered theirs; if Terry needed a computer or a shoulder to lean on, she knocked on my door.

One Sunday afternoon, Anita rang my bell in jeans, a big man's shirt, no make-up, and her hair piled up and held on top of her head with a rubber band, but off-center. She offered me a beautiful slice of lemon cake, with lemon curd between the layers and delicately scented buttercream icing piped in a perfect curl on top. That week she took off from her job, and over the next days she showed me her downy butter cake, the delicate crumb of her scones, and the elegant balance of her tart and sweet fruit pastries. I told her what seemed obvious: She was a talented baker. That simple praise propelled her off Wall Street and into Peter Kump's New York Cooking School.

Of course she excelled: she was passionate, clearly reaching for her dream. We began to speak more often while she was in school. She showed me samples from her classes, and I asked her to do specialty baking for events I was booked to cater. After completing her training, she took jobs as a pastry chef in several high-end restaurants to continue to learn, and she helped bake and serve in my catering business as she tried to launch her own scone business.

Then she was ill a few times, and I didn't know all the details, but her bouts with Crohn's disease and irritable bowel syndrome cost her a couple of jobs. She worked for me, filling in, while she sought her next position. At one of them, she met Irwin, a chef.

In the following years, she threw herself into her two big loves: baking, and her relationship with this strange man. He took her away from jobs (all bosses sucked), her apartment down the hall (there were cheaper/better places to live), her roommate Terry (no time for her friends), and working for me (don't work for anyone but yourself). After sharing an apartment in midtown for a while, Anita and Irwin moved to a place in New Jersey, where good baking jobs were even harder for her to find and Irwin could not locate trustworthy employers.

He changed her worldview and her style, seemed to influence everything she did—and how much debt she incurred. Terry would ask if I had seen her; I would ask if Terry had heard from her. Neither of us had frequent contact, but when we did see her, she was always very, very sad. She loved Irwin deeply, with great empathy and kindness; "The rest of the world be damned," she said, and she meant it.

She let me buy her coffee one wintery afternoon. We met down near Astor Place, where she told me she had a "program" to attend and I had a few errands nearby. She was late and, when she did show up, looked as though she had been out in the rain a long time, perhaps commuting in from New Jersey. Her grand hair was tucked into an over-sized Rastafarian sock hat, colorful and crocheted full of dramatic textures channeled from Chihuly glass works. She explained, "I'm knitting and crocheting items to attract buyers to this used-goods website, where I sell some of my other stuff." She was not specific about the website or what she was selling, but two moves removed from our building, I was pretty sure she had not carted many heirlooms along, so selling what remained in her possession did not sound good to me. She told me how things stood with Irwin: He was not going to live for long.

Anita helped Irwin deal with his final, debilitating illness. She took care of him in their apartment, hidden away from everyone. She gave him the ever-increasing dosages of morphine when he couldn't reach for the pills himself. And after he was gone, when the debts compounded, the Crohn's disease and IBS overwhelmed her gut, and her sixtieth birthday loomed with no job prospects and no health insurance, she had enough pills left to lace her own last Diet Coke.

Some of us are given more in life than others. Some of us have the heart and courage to grab for more than the portion we *are* given, and some of us leave behind gifts sweeter than the lives we lived. It's Anita's banana cake, included in my cookbook, and her honey madeleine (below), that I bake when I need a taste to trigger deep thoughts of those tender and intense people, my catering crew.

Honey Madeleines

Mix together with a whisk or spatula in a large mixing bowl:
  2 large eggs
  5 tablespoons sugar
  1 tablespoon dark brown sugar
  Pinch of salt
  Optional, ¼ tsp. vanilla extract

Mix together in measuring cup:
  ¾ cup flour
  1 teaspoon baking powder

Add honey to warm butter and stir together:
  6 tablespoons butter, melted
  1 tablespoon honey

Melt to coat madeleine pans:

2 tablespoons butter

Gently fold flour and baking powder into egg mixture,. Blend in melted butter and honey just until mixed—*Do Not Beat It.*

Cover with plastic wrap and leave in cool place for 30 minutes.

Preheat oven to 425 degrees.

Generously grease pans with 2 tablespoons melted butter.

Spoon about 1 tablespoon of flour, egg, and honey mixture into each madeleine form (fill halfway) and bake about 10 minutes. Yield: One and one-half dozen delicate cakes.

Tap upside down onto rack or counter to cool. They will fall out by themselves!

All I Ask Of You

"All I ask of you is
forever to remember me as loving you..."
   —Gregory Norbert, OSB, Weston Priory

ICHAEL DIED THE LAST WEEK of December 1989. He was sorry not to live to see the new decade. He was sorry not to see. . .so much.

I urged him to go to Spain in 1988, even as parasites began to overwhelm his gut. In 1989, his last summer, I insisted he take some money and use it, as a "fun fund." He wouldn't live long enough to benefit from a retirement plan (as if my small business could ever have offered him one!). I wanted him to take what money there was and do whatever he could, while he could. He wanted to visit a friend in Los Angeles and see Disneyland. But his friend spent most of the time at his job. Disneyland was too exhausting, not much fun without kids along. There was so much more he had hoped to experience, like a solid and loving relationship, watching his nieces and nephews grow up, more travel. He was thirty-five, and we couldn't imagine how little time was left, how little energy.

A few years before, those bright blue eyes sparked directly at me. They were pure energy beams flashing with such intensity from the top of a long, lithe body. He came to interview at the New York Restaurant School while I was the director. He was already sold on the program before he arrived, ready to start immediately. He eagerly explained himself: his math degree, early-childhood education minor, and years working service in a corporate dining room. Could he qualify for admission to this program? I barely managed my sales pitch, he was talking so fast, so excited by everything he was seeing and smelling as we toured the kitchens. I knew if the faculty could tap into his energy, he would be an extraordinary student.

Just as he began school, I stopped directing the program and was enrolled myself as a student in the course. After a first, quizzical look at me in my white chef's jacket, he sat down next to me, expecting me to lead the orientation. He started conversation, politely asking about which way to hold the knife. I said, "Avoid the blade." And then he got it. Someone else began the orientation speeches, and I was no longer the director to be buttered up; I was classmate and colleague with whom to compete.

Michael gobbled up the workload, impressed the teachers, and competed at every task. He was quick-witted, always processing many thoughts out loud, walking/talking, developing his restaurant proposal assignment. He rattled out answers before the faculty had finished the questions, and challenged them with his next questions, not satisfied with partial answers; he wanted more. In an immaculate uniform, he was the first into the kitchens in the morning; he checked inventory, rotated and dated goods, cleaned out the nasty back corners of refrigerators —any task he could find, he did before the faculty could ask.

We worked, laughing and pushing each other to excel as we competed our way through the training. I knew I was opening my own catering business as soon as I graduated and wanted him as chef/partner. I saw a champion as we fed one another, drove one another to give just a bit more, just a little more. I felt his buzzing energy when he entered a room. It excited (or exhausted!) everyone around him. I fed off his energy: was it electrodes or kinetic-body-energy? I didn't understand, but I responded to him. He loved big, bright red Gerber daisies and took photos of bunches of them, planning to decorate the walls of his own restaurant with them someday.

He went right from school to work in the Bridge Café under Chef Leslie Revsin, who had been the first woman chef at the Waldorf Astoria. Tough as they come, she was a strong, assertive kitchen commander. She would ask him for a case of roasted peppers, and they'd be done, labeled, and in the walk-in before she realized he had started the prep. He was born to it, with an intuitive sense of handling foods; hands that made the chix tear out their own breastbones, peel off their skins, and lie down flat on his cutting board, ready for whatever he wanted to do with them.

Just a few months out of school, he worked faster than three typical kitchen staff. No equipment was too big, too hot, or had too much power for him; he loved a cranked-up eight-burner stove! Two years out of culinary school, he was on top of his game, ready to lead a high-quality kitchen. And he *did* get to be chef in his own kitchen, the first half year of 1989. But then he came down with pneumonia, and the parasites again. He had to be hospitalized for a while and had to give up the chef position, never got to the spotlights that shone on star chefs in the 1990s.

He tried to work with me that fall. I had several parties, and I asked him to come and prep with us, not work the parties—that was too long a day for him by then—but to prep a few hours, get us ahead of schedule, be with us. Bobby and Max and Lilia and I all knew the score. We were all crossing off dozens of names from our address books that year. We wanted to keep Michael up, going, living as long as possible. For years, when he stood up at the stove, we were merely prep-machines, puttering along, with his roiling, boiling engine in gear.

But no more. He was in slo-mo for a few minutes, then needed to lie down. No one had a problem with him lying down on the sofa to rest every little while, but he had sweats, he was dizzy, lost his balance.

In late October, after Michael spent most of his hours resting on the sofa, he picked up his knife roll and walked out. He weaved toward the elevator. I walked with him, murmuring empty reassurances. I asked him to call when he got home, off the subway, three long blocks west to his apartment on Twenty-third Street, up the five flights. I wanted to know he had made it, but I did not trust his strength to keep him independent anymore, and I wasn't sure what was needed next. He got onto the elevator and I came back into the kitchen and cried, just cried.

It was his last day working with us. His shoulder-length curls were falling out, his fireball energy was gone, the intense performance was over. Lilia poured me a cup of tea, Bobby and Max kept prepping, talking me through, hands busy and eyes averted, speaking of so many others they knew. AIDS was such a plague on our community.

That was the late '80s, the worst of the wipe-out. AIDS devastated my staff, everyone's. Caterers all had to decide: Do we let a dying man pass our precious hors d'oeuvres? Do we hide our favorite staff doing paper work? How long *can* he work before he looks too sick? Before he collapses at a gig? Before he makes someone else sick? How do you *not* hire someone who's worked loyally for you six, eight, ten years?

Just a few years earlier, the story had been so different. These handsome men, all of them too gorgeous for me to ever approach at a party when I was a teenager, were happy to work for me. It was a trip for me to get to "play" with them: jokes and food and teasing about lookers/hookers and the party clothes and dissing the ladies, as those sweet young things coveted the men's beautiful tuxedo-clad bods. Many of the men weren't "out" yet. Their Gay Pride was best expressed at the once-a-year Halloween Parade through Greenwich Village. Young girls didn't know what was going down, but I was old enough and trusted, so I got to see some of the real heat exchanged in the kitchen. Then things changed so much, so fast.

Michael did call that day when he got home, and sporadically over the next few days. Sometimes he was coherent; sometimes he wasn't quite lucid. I urged him to see his doctor, go to his support group; what were his plans for Thanksgiving? He wasn't really clear about that, so I offered to drive him to his mom's in Connecticut. I had to get down to the meat market, pick up my own turkey, and I would pick him up and drive him to Ridgefield; we would have some time just to talk. A few days later, he seemed reluctant but agreed to the plan.

He was very weak and tired as we drove north the Wednesday before Thanksgiving. I hoped sharing the holiday with his family would be a good idea, but they weren't real happy to have him around. Seven siblings, partners, their children, and his mom gathered for the feast. Afterward, someone dropped Michael off at the bus terminal, so he had to get back to the city on his own. That Monday, on the phone, he told me how he'd washed his own dishes, had had to separate his laundry, that no one had wanted to sit next to him. It made him so very sad. He was so alone; he was afraid.

A few days later, his phone was knocked out. Maybe he pulled the plug hoping to die in his own bed, but I didn't want the police to find him and take him to St. Vincent's. I had been there with him before, and he told me he wanted to go to Cabrini Hospital, if necessary, where his doctor was affiliated. I had to get that small request honored by the EMS crew. It was the first week of December, and I couldn't leave the kitchen to get to his apartment: In a couple of hours, I had to be in Hoboken, New Jersey, creating a surprise anniversary party I had booked months before. I reached Michael's roommate at his work, before we left with the party. I asked him to check on Michael, get him to Cabrini if necessary. He was a nice guy, too appalled by the scene to get very involved, but he did what I asked.

When I got to see Michael, finally, the next morning, he was still in the ER, lying in his own filth. I cried so hard, standing in the middle of Cabrini Hospital Emergency Room, that someone came to clean him up, check his vitals, and calm me down. I think he was close to comatose. It took a while for him to recognize me, to see the bright red Gerber daisies I had brought, to tune in to my voice.

When they finally found him a bed and rolled him away, a social worker approached me, offered to help. I will always remember her kindness through the wet haze of that ER. How do you help someone mourn as the shock waves of grief roll in? I knew Michael would not leave the hospital. Few people came to see him in those last days. I saw him once more when he was able to speak to me, with such a fine gift of words: "You are the best friend I've ever had. You are the best friend."

I treasure the two photos Michael gave me, one as he posed sitting on an ancient stone wall in Madrid, and another as he leaned against Antonio Gaudi's tiled blue dragon in Park Guell overlooking Barcelona. They had been taken just sixteen months earlier, with his glorious, flamboyant curls still gracing his shoulders, his eyes direct, looking right back at you. He left money for his own funeral, and he chose the hymn he wanted sung by a friend for his memorial service, which I led, as he asked.

All I ask of you, is forever to remember me, as loving you.

       Deep the joy of being together in one heart,
    and for me that's just where it is.

       As we make our way through all the joys and
    pain, can we sense our younger, truer selves?

Someone will be calling you to be there for a while.

Can you hear the cry from deep within?

Laughter, joy and presence: the only gifts you are.

Have you time? I'd like to be with you.

       Persons come into the fiber of our lives, and
    then

       their shadow fades and disappears.

All I ask of you, is forever to remember me as loving you.

That Big Paper Bag

THE FIRST GIG MAX WORKED FOR ME was the night I fired Les so we could stay married. The three of us were catering a second-marriage wedding for sixty adults in a spectacular apartment on Central Park West. I was in the kitchen, coaxing the maid into permitting me to cook on her immaculate stove, to actually use the kitchen, while Les and Max were serving champagne and hors d'oeuvres, wandering through a dozen rooms in tuxedoes. This was early in my work catering, and I had hired Les because I didn't know many men who owned tuxedoes. His was still fresh from our wedding two months earlier. While I had planned, prepped, organized, and delivered that event, for some two hundred guests, once I changed into the wedding gown his mother found on a bride in France and "borrowed" for me to wear, and Les was in his tuxedo, my staff, mostly former classmates, worked the gig. Max was a friend of one of my classmates who had helped with our wedding, then taken a full-time job as chef at a local breakfast spot. He was not available for this event, but he knew Max had a tuxedo.

Once the cocktails were rolling out, flower-garnished trays all set, I concentrated on my timing for dinner. The bride had insisted on a finicky dish, shrimp in cream sauce on boneless chicken breasts. Bright green asparagus were the only contrast to the creamy colors of the food, table dressing, and candlelit room she chose. Timing was important, as the sauce had to reduce but not so far that it broke. The precepts of nouvelle cuisine at the time prohibited using cornstarch to bind the sauce, and I was relying on the guys to cue me when the guests were ready for dinner.

First Max came in and told me, "Fifteen minutes."

Then Les arrived to say, "Hurry up, they're ready!"

Max came back and said, "Slow it down—they took another round of champagne and are still interested in the hors d'oeuvres I just passed."

I was cranking up the heat, rushing to meet the pace and then turning it down to hold for "relaxed" and gracious timing, while growing frantic at the idea of the sauce breaking as it hit the cool serving platter with that maid watching. Then Les came back in and *ordered* me, "Hurry it up!"

I listened to Max. After all, no one was rushing off to a business meeting, and no one would starve if they waited another few minutes for dinner. Max was experienced at this timing. Tall and handsome in his tuxedo, he told me what he noticed about the room appointments, and I understood he enjoyed working the crowd as much as he enjoyed talking me down from my apparent frenzy.

At the end of the evening, when the glowering maid pushed the floor mop into my hands, Max quickly took it from me, without asking or being asked, and coaxed the maid away. After the party, I of course fired Les, so we are still married, and Max became my Main Man.

MAX WORKED FOR ME PRETTY STEADILY after that party, and when I needed help shopping at Fairway a few years later, he came over early and pitched right in. We started with a two-hour grocery list tutorial.

I explained the list to Max: the ripeness required for the cherry tomatoes we were going to stuff just before service, the size and count I wanted for each of seven hors d'oeuvre items, all with multiple moving parts, in quantities sufficient for seventy-five guests, to prep on Wednesday. When Max finally got to Fairway, it was the longest shopping expedition of his life, but he shopped to my specifications; he was careful with each choice, quantities, and my money.

Max was there, at my side, helping me through so many corporate cocktail parties, housewarmings, kids' parties, private dinners and public free-for-all events for fifteen years, meeting me for grocery shopping in the early mornings, standing next to me prepping while practicing his tap routines.

"Hey, is that dill done, Max? Don't make a career out of it! I like that extra brush before the left toe tap." He washed the stacks of dirty pots and utensils, rehearsed me as I talked myself through event timing, over and over again. Max is a performance artist: a dancer, he is musical, witty, has great timing and grace under pressure. He is a sweet and gentle soul.

But one raw January morning, I knew for certain what other staff had been telling me and I didn't want to hear.

We had been hired to create an ornate "English Tea" to be served at 8:00 a.m. as a gifts-and-accessories firm launched its big video sales presentation, packed with droning facts of code numbers, pricing, and counts per box. To start off their show-room week, I asked Max to help me, in the basement meeting room of the Design and Decorators Building. This was a building from the Gilded Age, ornate on the outside but hollowed out floor by floor, converted to less glorious purposes, with show-room on showroom of *chachkas* for sale upstairs, display upon display of "collectibles."

Our food was supposed to motivate the sales staff to go forth and sell their English-themed collectibles to store owners nationwide, hoping these items would be prominently displayed in lots and lots of retail store windows and, urged on by corpo-rate incentives, the store sales staff would then sell lots and lots of them to the public. Apparently, to decorate their homes, people bought and displayed these "collectibles": miniature statues; replicas of porcelain dolls once hand-painted in Euro-pean shops, now mass-produced in China; chrome-plated candy dishes, made-to-look-like-real-silver; machine cut-glass dishes; doll-sized dishes; snow-cone paper weights. Dust collectors, all of them.

We would offer drinks and treats to ease the sales staff through the tedium of their days during the showroom week. For these sales weeks, I usually hired trained dancers and models. They supported sales by feeding the wholesale buyers, smiling at everyone, and breaking nothing. Lithe and agile, they could navigate the fragile displays of breakables while balancing trays of delicacies, drinks, and beverage napkins. They were all gorgeous young people. (I didn't know one had modeled nude in a gay men's magazine just a month before!) They labored hard, carefully, and cheerfully as the English Tea theme was carried through the week, everyone friendly and chatty as they worked the showroom formally decked out in full tuxedoes.

The first morning, car service deposited Max and me, along with our boxes of my handmade scones and cucumber sandwiches, jams and clotted cream, at the service entrance to the Designers and Decorators Building. We had worked there before, so we joked easily with Eddie, the elevator operator, and promised him breakfast as he helped us haul everything into the back of the basement meeting room, just outside the kitchen alcove folding doors. I landed the food on the two-foot-square counter space allotted for catering, and Eddie located the cases of rented polished silver service, delivered the day before and locked away in a storage space. The company officers, led by Brad with a cartload of computer video equipment, arrived to set up their slide show.

One minute Max was standing just behind me, pulling the plastic wrap off silver samovars, candelabra, clean white linens, china, and tiny silver spoons. The next moment, he was kneeling down, fishing around beneath his tux in that big paper bag, his hands shaking. I saw him pull out his Poland Spring bottle. I watched him take a sip, and I saw his hand steady. Then the gentle gray eyes, not quite pleading, caught mine. He looked away fast, mumbled about having all the required rentals. With my eyes averted, I pressed some cash into his hand and sent him out into the bracing air for a couple of bags of ice at the corner deli. As my hands stacked the scones up neatly and the jams glistened primly in the silver bowls filled three quarters' inch below the rim, I tried to gauge what had just happened, what response I ought to have.

When I placed the silver candelabra on a white-clothed table to catch a spotlight, I winked at Brad, who was fussing with the slide show. He smiled comfortably over at me and asked no questions. He figured I had things well in hand, but his slides were not coming along in the sequence he wanted. I muttered a "thank goodness" under my breath, grateful he was distracted, and grateful for his trust. I was glad that I had the food ready and the service equipment was all there. I scooted to the back of the room to finish opening the plates, cutlery, and napkins to add to the table presentation.

After fifteen years working together, I had a pretty good idea of how long it should take Max to get to a deli and return with two bags of ice. Perhaps it was morning coffee rush hour and the cash registers were backed up? Perhaps he had to find a second deli?

The water was boiling in my five-gallon urn, ready to transfer into the three silver samovars, but I was a bit nervous about handling those hot containers by myself. The table wasn't quite set yet. Usually Max helped me move the heavy equipment and finished the table details, lining up the cutlery and plates precisely at just the right distance from the edges of the table, making room for my food displays, before he changed into his tuxedo with fifteen minutes to spare. But that day he was out in the cold, looking for ice.

As the sales reps started to arrive, I had to get that table ready. I bit my lip, transferred some hot water into one samovar and brought it out on the floor myself. I went back and forth twice more, setting up the entire table display in an apron and chef's coat, not exactly the proper attire for a formal tea service.

Where was Max in his tuxedo? The graceful gentleman did not return as expected. I just kept setting up, tearing off plastic wrap at a furious pace, hustling to hide rental crates, pulling the folding doors closed so guests wouldn't see the chaos in the kitchen alcove. Panic seized my hands, moving fast, as I ticked off all the tasks to be completed in front of the house before a hundred fifty people arrived in the next ten minutes. Max was the performance artist, not me! He had never been so off in his timing, had always entered on cue, stage right, dressed perfectly in costume, when needed. Where *was* he?

Was I going to carry the event solo? At 8:00 a.m., they started the slides, but there weren't a hundred and fifty people out there. Perhaps the weather kept the sales people away, or they didn't give a damn about English-themed collectibles. I wasn't worried about the food—the company staff would happily eat the dozens of scones upstairs in the showroom, all week long. But how would I handle all the china and silver service, and empty the hot samovars? Where was Max?

He returned with the ice just before the slide presentation ended and changed into his tux just as the sales reps hit the buffet. I served them in my apron, half-hidden behind the triple-tiered cake stand, hoping the gleam of the silver would blind the guests to my harried, inappropriate appearance. All Max could do was hold himself erect, standing as a decorative accent at the edge of the table. Perhaps a dozen sales reps took their tea, grabbed scones, and split for their business day, hauling themselves around the building full of showrooms.

We cleared the tea table as Brad packed his slides and equipment. He took the service elevator back upstairs before we were done. He was gracious: "Carol, thanks for the lovely set-up. It's really just what we wanted. I'm looking forward to those scones upstairs, when I can taste them!" We chuckled together, easily. I would make sure Brad had extras of everything, in his office, on his own plate, to enjoy in quiet as he reviewed his sales activity reports, all week long.

I packed the clotted cream, jams, and finger sandwiches in plastic containers to set into the office refrigerator for the week's showroom hospitality, and filled other Rubbermaid tubs with scones and toast points that my crew could set on the counter, to be rifled by the staff as they sought snacks or lunch or relief from their days' frustrations. I set up breakfast for Eddie at the elevator. Max changed out of his tux and slowly helped me empty the samovars and bundle the linens and silver service back into the rental crates. Eddie took him express to the fifth floor showroom with the goodies while I loaded my tools into my boxes and rolled my dollies over to the service elevator, ready to leave as soon as Max came down. I knew he would put things away carefully, and I knew staff would leave something out on the counter during the day to spoil, but it didn't matter; I would bring replacements and freshly baked scones tomorrow. When Max came down, I hailed a taxi. Eddie grinned with delight at his breakfast and helped us to the curb.

I asked the driver to stop first at Max's home, and there would be no discussion of that decision. I spoke soothing niceties during the ride: "Ooo, it's too cold to be out on the street! Do you feel like a flu coming on, Max?" I assured him I could certainly manage to unpack and get on with my preparations alone for the rest of the week; although we had planned for him to help me two more days, I assured him the weather would keep the crowd small. I told him to "feel better" as he got out of the cab. I handed him the big paper bag containing his tuxedo and the Poland Springs bottle. He would need the tuxedo for another performance, but he would not work for me again.

POSTSCRIPT: THE NEXT MONTH I DROVE Max to HighWatch, a rehab facility in western Connecticut. Every morning now, Max decides again to be clean and sober, as he has since that winter of 1994. We remain good friends as he continues his life as a successful, working performance artist.

Moving To
The Suburbs

1999–2020

Catering 9/11/01

OLD FRIENDS HAD LOST a new son-in-law. My food industry friends found themselves feeding hundreds of firemen, EMTs, and volunteers. I had closed my business five years earlier but received calls to cater memorial services. I forget how many. All anyone said was, "Please do it," and all I said was, "What time? Where?" No one knew how many would attend.

This service was at the Little Church, a hospitable Episcopalian congregation that simply made its space available to all who asked following 9/11. But their small staff was overwhelmed by the simplest sanitation needs of the flood of mourners who passed through their doors for so many memorial services. Their reception room was small, there was no real kitchen for preparing food, and the area was a shambles when I arrived. The clergy, in full vestment, were pushing brooms. The houseman, washing out a coffee urn, asked if this and that belonged to me. I had just arrived, but I could not ask him for logic. I stepped in and did what was needed.

My friends are Jewish, their daughter had converted to Catholicism, and the new in-laws were Anglican. The friends set out Glen's summer hiking boots, joyful photos of early vacations, and a signature book for the young widow to review later on, for what comfort might lie in the show of strength-in-numbers. Whose custom is that?

Young men brought in coolers of iced beer and wine; young women were decorating with thick, sparkling gold ribbons, votive candles, and burgundy table linens—acts of kindness for their lost friend. A few plates were left on the table, potluck. My friends asked me to bring boiled eggs, salt, and a circular cake: symbolic foods for a shiva to comfort the Jewish mourners.

Someone set out the top layer of the couple's wedding cake, frozen just four months earlier, that they had intended to share on their first anniversary, which now would never happen. Whose custom is *that*?

When the service began, I peeped into the chapel, standing half-hidden behind a black curtain. There were many widows in black, every seat was taken, and the side aisles were filled. I heard the widow's young son read a good-bye speech to his stepfather against a backdrop of organ music and copious crying. The press noted that everyone who had worked at, or whose loved one had worked at, Cantor-Fitzgerald attended all the services. For months, hundreds of friends, colleagues, families—equally bereft—came out to service after service, funeral after funeral. There was no way to estimate the crowds, no way to guess how many would appear for the service, then leave, or how many would stay for food, drink, and an effort at conversation afterward. They just came out for one another, a notable expression of corporate etiquette.

I arranged the foods I had brought, the plates set on the table, and those handed to me. I set scoops in the ice, loosened wine corks, and left openers easily accessible on the table edge. I fanned the beverage napkins, opened stacks of plastic cups, then stepped back out of the way as the crowd flowed into the reception space when the chapel service ended.

My friends were quiet, their backs against the black drape that hid the reception service area chaos, watching their tall and beautiful daughter in a black lace mantilla, braced by friends at her side, receive the greetings of Glen's former colleagues and their families. Glen's parents stood there as well, elderly and frail, their sorrow acknowledged only occasionally, eclipsed by the young widow's.

In the legal wrangling and bizarre settlements of the following months and years, the 9/11 Commission gave the widow compensation for the loss of her husband. Communication ended with her in-laws as they mourned their only child and slipped quietly away from these newest relations. Whose custom was that?

By Thanksgiving, the widow had a new life, cut off from her own parents as well as her son, who was left in the custody of his father. She was convinced everyone wanted something from her that she was unable to give, and the distance grew over the years. Occasional e-mails, and an annual luncheon with her father, petered out over the years. Calls to her son ended long before he began college. So much broke apart in the collapsed rubble of the Towers; we still don't know everything.

There is an annual recognition of the 9/11 losses at the memorial reading of names. The world has not found enough customs to comfort itself through more terrorist attacks. We all light candles, bring flowers, feed one another in the effort to move forward, but the toll of these events is a calculus beyond understanding.

September 11, 2001: Orasri Liangthanasarn

ORASRI WAS MISSING? She never missed a chance to see, to taste, to smile. She never missed a question, a challenge, a new task.

Orasri used her curiosity: She sponged up ideas, responded eagerly, respectfully, said "thank you!" and laughed with a sweet, bouncing, and sincere joyfulness.

Orasri chose a shimmering yellow Thai silk scarf for me. Yellow—a sensuous yellow the color of our little ribbons commemorating war heroes. It was a precious, rare gift, made more precious in that it won't be followed with the exchange of others. I gave her tastes of cookies and catering, ideas and encouragement. I reveled in her lively enthusiasm.

SHE WAS SO GOOD AT WHAT SHE DID: She was that charmed statistic, the intern so good she was hired by her sponsor. *Orasri was just that good.*

She was happy and excited to be working on top of the

world, right where she wanted to be. She earned it, she was grateful for the opportunity, and she was delighted with her first success.

Orasri is no longer missing. But many of us will miss her for a long, long time.

—*Carol G. Durst*
Adjunct, Department of Nutrition and Food Studies
New York University

Suburban Dislocation

NEARLY HAD AN AUTO ACCIDENT every trip to the local A&P.
Although I can hold my own lane against New York City taxi
drivers, and have driven a fifteen-foot U-Haul truck up and
down the New York State Thruway and across midtown Manhattan, I brushed the side rails more than once when these suburban ladies maneuvered their Navigators, BMW Wagons, and
Mountaineers head-on at me astride the double yellow lines.

About a year into our relocation, there came an evening
when I threw Will into my car, driving south, then transferred
him in Yonkers to my husband driving north, back to our house,
as I drove on into the City. While he cooperated, I knew it wasn't
a good way for any kid to spend an evening. That night, with
time pressing on me and no way to assess the traffic both my
husband and I faced, it became clear to me that not many catering gigs were worth crossing six lanes of rush-hour traffic with
a kid. It was a hard choice: I had to let go of my catering business in the city as I tried to acculturate to the suburbs.

But I was an alien in that foreign land, where my food and food knowledge, which I thought was my strongest language of communication, the language I used so proficiently in New York City, didn't work. No passport was required to move to the suburbs, but perhaps I really needed one. The manners and customs did not match the ways I had known all my life in New York, just thirty-five miles south.

I still had a catering-driven urge, a need to feed and work with food, but I could not cater for the parents of my son's classmates, not in such a status-driven community. I could not have his classmates see me use the kitchen entrance to their homes: I would be setting Will up to be tormented, bullied, by his peers.

Attending various PTA meetings, I met with attitudes reflecting intense class distinctions: those moms taking time from work as attorneys, accountants, and financial planners had a different view of my "dirty" work in kitchens. I found much greater acceptance when I described myself as university faculty. In fact, I seemed an object of great communal interest when I said I taught in the Department of Nutrition and Food Studies. My professional training as a chef, my years of catering and running my own business, even my credential as a cookbook author and food stylist, possessed no caché in their affluent world. Most of them moved a few feet further away from me in any public space, and they changed seats in private homes once they thought I could actually show them how to use their spotless, high-end kitchen equipment. As a faculty member, I achieved an intellectual gravitas and social status they were more comfortable having around. In their community, people write checks they contribute to worthy causes, but they are a long way from the shoulder-to-shoulder effort of the old- fashioned community barn-raising in the formerly Quaker village they occupy.

When I tried to teach an after-school program, "What's for Dinner?" at the local middle school, cooperating with another mother, I learned more about the strange attitudes toward food, and toward those who prepared it from scratch. My students made so many suggestions about where to buy prepared foods, I think they felt sorry for me, working to blend salad dressing with a whisk. Several stood back from the brownies, even the written recipes, as though the paper contained a voodoo that would instantly make them fat. My co-teacher, ostensibly trained in nutrition in her native India, would only propose items concocted of condensed milk, marshmallow, and mango puree—or fruit smoothies based on premium ice cream. She didn't think the kids would be interested in tasting different kinds of rice, yogurt-based sauces, or how to turn left-over chicken into a curry. Probably, she was right on that last one: In that neighborhood, leftovers were dumped immediately into the garbage.

Neighbors

Neighbors on both sides of our house didn't warm to our arrival. One, an elderly woman who shared our forked driveway, lay in wait for me, hidden behind the bushes. When I approached in my car, she jumped out and, face to the car window, hissed "Son of a bitch! Scum of the earth!" It was several very long years before her family moved her to assisted living.

When we first bought our house, intending to use it only on weekends, Will was an infant. We walked over to meet the neighbors on the other side. Another senior couple, they told us to call before we came over again. About twelve years later, police knocked on my door, asking what I might know about a robbery at their home, since I'd had *immigrant construction workers* around my house at that time. I knew nothing. Eventually, the police arrested someone working with the neighbors' lawn service. Then I broke the rule, again: Without calling first, I baked a banana cake and brought it over, saying how sorry I was for the break-in. They put their house up for sale.

It was a long walk to other neighbors, who mostly drove away from their homes. I'm not sure they ever saw me coming, but it seemed they were rarely home.

Claire

The first year we moved to our ritzy suburban community full-time, I tried to hold onto my catering business and my free-lance food work in the city. So when I got to the check-out counter at the local A&P, my groceries were often of odd assortment and quantity.

Claire noticed. "What do ya do with all that? Looks like you do a lot of baking," she ventured to say one day. She made me think of Mrs. Santa Claus with her rosebud mouth, lipsticked a cheerful red, in full pink cheeks. As she looked up at me, her gray eyes twinkled. Her question was not intrusive. I explained what I was up to and found her willing to tell me a lot about herself over the years.

"I don't do much baking—it's about all I can do to get some food on the table, get the grandkids off to their activities. There's always someone coming and going, so food just has to be at the table when they are, and lots of it! Boy, can they eat! My husband and I marvel at how much and how fast groceries disappear! And the next thing you know, I'm shopping for more food again! It never stops!"

Over the years, I gathered her husband was disabled, her daughter's husband wasn't around, her daughter worked some-times, and there were three grandkids always eating at her table.

"I've got to rush home today, get the middle one to soccer practice, then fix some dinner and take my granddaughter to her ballet class. Then I've got to pick him up from soccer, go back and get her, and get home to clean up the dishes. Boy, I can't wait to see my pillow tonight! Ya know, just when ya think they're all lined up, doing what they're supposed to be doing, *bam!* One of them acts up, right? My daughter has to run to the school: another meeting with a teacher. Boy, it doesn't stop, does it?"

Claire survived several changes in A&P management, dress code, and procedures. I always waited out her line, knowing she would find something upbeat to say in her assessment of the la-test changes. "Ya know, when management can't figure out what to do, they just change things around—then everyone gets so mixed up, and they all feel better when they go back to how things were, all sorted out again! Nothing's fixed!" she con-cluded with a chuckle, wagging her head.

Once, my purchases provoked the observation, "Either you

really like beans or you're making something special for a lot a people!" I explained to her I would be demonstrating weights and measurements, the use of kitchen scales, and what happens when dry beans are measured against cooked ones for a class of food service workers who didn't really understand much about math.

She responded vehemently, "Ya know, I was *terrible* in math! The nuns used to tell me I was just too stupid to get math and I should take a commercial program, not go for the harder courses, for college-prep, you know? Boy, did they ever make me feel like the lowest of the low!"

I mentioned the studies where girls were (and still are) turned off to math and science and therefore eliminated from so many careers and opportunities to earn good money.

"Yeah, you can say that again! Boy, was I ever turned off! I wonder what the old dames would say now, to see me punching numbers all day long, cashing out at the end of the day! Ha!" Although she didn't say this with bitterness, Claire's laugh was a mirthless bark. I could imagine how much math she handled in her life those days, leaving the cash register to go home and stretch a budget to feed at least six people out of her salary. I just stood there a bit longer, holding up the line, to speak my mind, letting her know it happened, and still happens, to too many people going through our education system.

"Oh, don't start me on that! I have a lot to say about how we educate young people today! Boy-o-boy, do I!" She was quite ready to go into it, but the line was getting longer, and my neighbors didn't appreciate my opinions, concerned as they were with whether their kids would go to Harvard or Yale, so Claire and I promised to discuss that at another time.

The day I loaded the conveyor belt with a hundred dollars' worth of frozen vegetables, she cocked her head and gave me the most mischievous look. "I didn't think you used so much frozen stuff. You always come through with the fresh fruits and vegetables. What's up?"

When I told her she would see photos of the very same packages in the following week's *Daily News* Food Section, she giggled and said, "Remind me to buy the paper that day— something interesting in it, instead of all the killings!"

We talked about setting up the photo shoot. She understood: It's a living. "Just so the food doesn't get wasted after the photos." I hated to waste perfectly good food, too. I assured her I would make it all into vats of soup and stews for the food pantry (serving a good segment of Northern Westchester), which was less than a mile from our house.

Claire was always the first cashier to open at the A&P, starting to deal with customers promptly at 7:00 a.m., and often I was in the store shortly after that. She told me she left her home upstate about 5:30 to get to work on time and her shift ended around 2:30 or 3:00 p.m. so she could get home for the grandkids. Sometimes her husband would cover for a little while, to allow her time to take care of errands on her way home. We laughed the most in those early-morning conversations, before customers lined up to purchase after-school snacks for the Brownie troop, or the last-minute, already-prepared dinner items, and we never tried to talk when those huge, overloaded carts rolled up. We both understood everyone was way too impatient for any polite conversation on their way home from the gym, the nail salon, and therapy.

Claire had such a clear sense of herself. She worked with great pride and competence, reached out to many of her customers, and chatted cheerfully as she fingered those register buttons. She was the most memorable character I met in suburbia in those early years. Certainly, she was the sweetest link in my Westchester food chain.

PTA

So yeah, I was a New York City food industry professional displaced to Westchester County, imprisoned for years of renovations inside my suburban containment unit, among neighbors who would not speak to me for lots of hideous reasons. I imagined that trying to work with PTA committees would be a place a professional food worker *could* be a welcome community member, contributing organizational skills, food preparation skills, and hospitality experience. Or, not. I was kicked off the PTA Hospitality Committee for attempting to retrieve someone's family heirloom silver service from a garbage bag, and from the Nutrition Committee for objecting to another member's plan to remove all foods her child was allergic to from district-wide school menus.

Transplanted to the burbs, I was not making an easy transition. I knew there must be nice people around—thinking, caring, sophisticated people who shared my values and interests —but I hadn't found them. Will brought home a few new friends, and I sought out their parents; I tried to connect. One small boy, invited over for a first playdate, devoured a large plate of home-made chocolate chip cookies, then kindly tried to give me directions to the nearest bakery, assuming I baked because I couldn't find my way there yet. Never mind that Simon & Schuster had just published my book on desserts.

I attended a PTA gathering and found one woman who liked to cook. She also liked the fact that, when I said I would do something, actually did it, and that I would clean up as well. She invited me to join the Hospitality Committee at the elementary school.

She was the Chair, and she wasn't too bitter about the lack of cooperation from the other committee members who signed up for the titles and perks, such as they were. I always showed up and did whatever needed doing while most of the other moms were busy schmoozing teachers, checking themselves out in the mirrors, protecting their nails, and recommending bargains and easy recipes. After years of catering, assisting with staff luncheons and PTA meetings meant I barely flexed my culinary muscles.

At the end of the year, the two of us went out for lunch. I hoped I had found a friend, but when our boys stopped talking to each other going into middle school the following year, our relationship abruptly ended as well.

She passed my name on to the Chair of Hospitality of the middle school, though, and I was invited to serve on the new committee. Since I had no competitive aspirations for leadership and tried to do as I was told, I was a useful member. I was given plenty of assignments to provide brownies, deliver beverages, return plates, and clean up throughout the year. I kept hoping that, if people saw my smiling face just a few more times, surely someone would respond to my comments or even begin a conversation with me.

In early spring, the Hospitality Committee Chair hosted a morning coffee meeting to plan the annual June celebration honoring the teachers and school staff. It was my big break! I had directions to one of the huge McMansions on the other side of town. I got there early, sat in my car watching the bright, clean snow melt off tree branches, and tried to talk myself into a cheerful demeanor. By the time a third brand-new SUV arrived in the driveway, I had rehearsed a pleasant-enough greeting and could muster a smile, so I got out of my car.

The Latina domestic opened the door and, eyes down, silently faded off stage-right as we all passed through the marble entry, left of the double-width curved stairway into the well-appointed kitchen: gleaming Sub-Zero, spotless top-of-the-line Wolfe six-burner with flattop, a major espresso machine and shiny new doodads all over the miles of counters, detailed tile work, Italian teardrop lighting, and a copper hood all in magazine-perfect placement. And, of course, there was the breakfast space. I couldn't call it a nook or an alcove: We were offered coffee in an area larger than my New York City apartment.

I reached for the coffee and took the skim milk. I didn't use Equal, and there was no sugar, no cream, on offer. I took a strawberry and quietly lectured myself: "Say nothing. You are not in charge here. Just do what you are asked to do—listen."

The next two hours were a detailed sociological study in how women fill time in the suburbs. All decisions were by committee, and every penny to be spent was discussed, in between tips on where to get haircuts, bargains on china pattern replacements, and a pool-cleaning service. I found myself drifting off to thoughts of client discussions and my own corporate board meetings, which I used to hold in my morning shower: I was president, vice president, secretary and treasurer of my catering corporation, and I made decisions way faster and bigger than the number of plastic water pitchers we ought to purchase. But I was in a different place, I told myself. I tried to be tactful. I tried to offer suggestions. And then I tried to keep quiet.

I didn't do such a hot job, though. By the time I left, I knew our hostess didn't really like me, and no one else looked up as I left. I had offered to bring my basic, utilitarian catering equipment to the luncheon, but that ran counter to the Chair's thoughts. She insisted everyone on the committee should bring their best china, preferably hand-painted faience and special serving utensils to make everything look glorious for the hard-working souls who took care of our children. The thought might be nice, but I didn't buy it: too many years of catering, I guess, watching too many platters shatter and expensive tools go missing. I tried to explain this, and when I left, I said I would bring the items I thought we might need, and if the committee didn't like them, I would just slip them under a table and bring them back home, no problem. I thought that was reasonable, but apparently it did not win me any friends.

The day of the Staff Appreciation Luncheon I got to the middle school and asked my son and a couple of his friends to help me carry my stuff up the three flights to the Teachers' Cafeteria. I bribed the kids with an offer of cookie tasting before the first bell rang for their classes. When we landed, it was apparent the teachers were not concerned with the cleanliness of their eating space and the other moms were not concerned with agreed-upon meeting times. The furniture needed rearranging to accommodate a buffet luncheon, and several parents had already dropped off their food contributions on the counter and tables, and left.

The boys went off to their day, and I began to clean and clear and drag tables into position as more and more food was dropped off. For an hour or so no other committee members appeared. Then, as they drifted in, they greeted each other and discussed what needed to be done. My commercial equipment was again rejected.

But as the numerous food contributions began to inundate us, the committee realized there was no other way to warm the dozens of aluminum foil pans full of cooked foods. As several members stood immobilized and others began to escalate into hysteria, I explained some basics of safe food handling, and then pulled my Sterno, hotel pans, and frames from under the tables, poured in boiling water from my unattractive coffee urn, and we continued, more safely, with our set-up. No chipped fingernails yet!

As the first teachers began to arrive to enjoy the fruits of parental labors, our Committee Chair arrived, shouting, "Look at my fabulous stuffed breast of chicken! Look at this, isn't this just gorgeous!" She stopped all preparations, demanding we attend to the huge, magnificent platter she claimed to have made, lovely mounds of chicken lined up and sauced to photo-shoot perfection. Everyone dutifully oo-ed and ahh-ed and then continued setting up the luncheon, chatting with the early-arriving faculty, getting the party going. Taking it out of a huge cardboard box, she placed her chicken where she thought it looked best, dead center, pushing other platters aside. The moms exchanged looks, but no one said anything; all we wanted was a pleasant event.

Teachers drifted in and out as the bells rang, the sounds of praise and pleasures filled the room, the hours passed, and we moved toward clean-up time. Since her chicken had been set out first, our Chair retrieved her platter early on and was ready to leave first. Although some of us understood we were to share in the clean-up, she replaced her tray in her huge cardboard box, closed the lid, and offered florid good-byes around the room. She left, marching out just as another mom asked if anyone had seen the silver serving fork she had brought along with her food and faience platter. She had her platter, but not this fork. It was an heirloom, from her mother-in-law. She began to ask more loudly about the fork, as it was not among the dishes and tools stacked on the counter.

My catering instinct kicked in: I grabbed two empty ice cube bags, put my arms into these "gloves" and dug into the garbage can at the entrance to the room. My committee colleagues stood back and watched me, aghast. Someone thought to ask the building maintenance staff to search through the two bags al-

| 221 |

ready removed from the room, but I knew that would prove use-less. By the time I reached to the bottom of this can, I knew the fork was not in the garbage and I knew where it was.

I was mad at myself for not finding a way to search that closed box as our Committee Chair was leaving. Was it possible that no one else realized what had happened? The woman would have to explain this loss to her husband and mother-in-law. I couldn't fathom her response, or rather her lack of re-sponse, after she asked a few times; she seemed calm, almost blasé. I thought how crazed I would have been in her shoes; it was precisely the reason I had suggested using my commercial equipment.

Everyone retrieved their platters and moved on to gather their kids and get home. My son and his friends came back up to see if there were any cookies left and to help me out with my equipment, now minus a few odd pieces like plastic bowls, side towels, and serving spoons I did not care about. I was appalled at the theft of someone's treasured serving piece, and although some of us had exchanged looks, it was not clear who under-stood what had happened. I finally realized that no one wanted to be thought rude enough to challenge another mother.

But then, no one from the committee spoke to me after that. I would get the barest nod if I crossed someone's path at the post office. I was not acknowledged by any of them at large PTA meetings or in the aisles of the A&P. I was not invited to the Hospitality Committee the following year, but I interpreted this as proof positive these suburbanites were so wealthy and so uncaring, what did it matter if someone's heirloom had disappeared into someone else's collection? So what?

I tried to tell myself, let it go, everyone else had. They did not like my commercial equipment, my arms in the garbage can, so I was off the committee.

I thought I was the only one disturbed by the thievery I had witnessed, and the incident just served to alienate me further from the community. But years later, after our kids had graduated from high school and left town for college, the woman who had lost her fork saw me at the bank, and for the first time (no one else was around), she spoke to me. "Do you believe what she did?" she hissed under her breath. "I know my fork is in her dining room right now, and I am so mad I don't know what to do about it!"

It was the first time anyone had acknowledged the incident to me. I was impressed with her candor: It was almost five years later, but she'd come right to the point. I told her it meant a lot to me that she knew what had happened, and we shared our rage and frustration that someone had stepped so far over the bounds of civil behavior.

She remembered how I'd reached into the garbage on her behalf, and she was still kicking herself for not finding some cute, charming way to have asked to see what was in the cardboard box. I told her I was disappointed not to have physically tackled the outrageous woman. I offered to scheme with her, to help recover her stolen fork. For the first time, I felt a connection with someone in suburbia. Odd that it was built on revenge.

The next year I was thrown off the PTA's Nutrition Committee, but that is another story primarily involving peanut butter.

Pork Loin and Latkes

OR THREE AND A HALF YEARS I lived in the suburbs during renovations. My husband drove off to New York City at 6:00 a.m., and my son climbed onto the school bus at 7:10. I could read after sending Will to school until the workers arrived, or after dark, after homework and dinner and loads of laundry—I washed towels I had laid down on our wooden floors to control the dust and debris tracked into the house—and answering the needs of who ever had called. My daily companions were hammers, drills, sanding machines, and a gang of Chilean immigrants. I don't speak Spanish. They didn't speak English. When they first arrived, their eyes revealed fears and unspeakable worries. I didn't know where, or how, they lived.

The project grew out of a three-month renovation of one room, adding another, and into a prolonged rebuilding of the entire house. When the workers sought to attach the one room to the rest of the structure, body-sized chunks of stucco broke off beneath the sledgehammer tapping at the corners. They showed me the rot caused by water dripping from the attic windows down through the walls between the interior rooms, still smoothly finished, and the insulation, now deteriorated mush, beams and studs rotted through.

At such a point, mid-December, most contractors would have taken a pass. Not Carlos; he faced it up. He shouldered deeper responsibility than most owners do: Nothing would be repaired with a slapdash patch. Problems would be fixed from the ground up. He signs his name to his work, unlike so many other Americans. He spoke softly with his crew, and they hunkered down to the tasks required, grateful to know there was steady work through the winter.

I gave up. I couldn't concentrate, couldn't write. My doctorate had to wait. The house was falling down, my husband was working in Europe, and decisions had to be made as, wall by wall, I could see collapse, rot, and instability. So I started to cook. I settled in to constant pounding and dumpsters being loaded ten hours a day. I began to make coffee, to set out water. Then I would set out a paper plate with cut-up fruit at the end of the day. Then I started to bake something to go with the morning coffee. Then I started to fix some sandwiches, then pasta, salads, soups, lentils, lentils with sausage, cakes, cakes. . . .

Six, sometimes eight, men climbed up and down scaffolding surrounding the house, peeled off chunks of stucco, stripped out wilted insulation, which they carried to a dumpster outside my office window, and then found ways to wedge fresh wood around decomposing window framing. It was an unplanned reconstruction on what we had thought was our sturdy little house, built in the 1920s.

One day the electric garage door died, but I could not stand to be outdoors, waiting for the next team of repairmen to arrive. The Chilean men had been out in the frigid air since daybreak. By mid-morning, I could see ice on the ladders, I could see their breath as they moved about, and I heard their syncopated music, but there was no place to be warm inside with the garage door stuck open. I drove to the A&P, looking for something to cook that would appease my own fears, my need to *do something* and distract myself from the image of the house falling down, my academic career ending before it began, our bank account sliding into the red zone. I found humble potatoes on the right side just as I entered the store, then pushed my cart to the meat counter at the rear. I avoided the middle aisles and stuck to the less-expensive basics on the outer edges: potatoes, onions, sour cream, apples, prunes, mustard, oil, pork loin.

Oh, about the pork loin: It is not in my family tradition, but as I realized I was about to share latkes from my culture, I wanted to reach across the continent and make something familiar to the workers as well. I hadn't counted on the Irish garage repair team arriving that day, but that's the good part about pork loin and potatoes, as Jack Ubaldi taught me early on: There's always enough to feed everyone, whoever is hungry when dinner is served.

It was even colder inside the house when I got back from the store. The garage and basement doors were *both* open then as the garage repairmen moved into the basement to change the mechanisms and test the automatic devices. The kitchen door was also open while the construction crew passed in and out to check whether the inner walls of the dining room were cracking or giving way to their pounding.

I lowered my grocery bags to the kitchen floor, jacked up the oven, and got busy. I kept quiet, with my fleece and jacket on, as I washed and ground ten pounds of potatoes and several large onions. While the pork loin roasted, coated with mustard and thyme, I fried a few dozen latkes and made a quick applesauce. I had some greens, so there was a salad. I made shallot vinaigrette to dress the greens and added a few apples and prunes to the pork roast. I opened the extension on the kitchen table, and the coffee was hot.

Henry Allen's garage repair workers had picked up their own hero sandwiches at Rocky's Italian Deli (they were several generations acculturated), so they ate their own lunch in the truck with the running engine warming them.

The Chileans were still working outside when I asked Carlos to bring them in to eat. The men walked around the house into the basement wash up sink, then came back outside to the kitchen door, seriously trying not to track mud and mess into the house. But no one came into the kitchen; their eyes were hungry, their noses twitching, but Carlos held tight reins on protocol. Only at his word, not mine, did they come in, take off their coats, sit down, and begin to eat. They talked softly; the Chilean accents were muted indoors, their music turned off outside. They paid attention to their plates, passed the platters of latkes, shared the meat, and reached for seconds. Clearly, they were glad to be sitting down for a bit and revived with hot food, a few tried some English sentences. They all managed "thank you" and I could answer "*de nada.*"

Here were immigrants becoming Americans. Over the months, Alex, Mauricio, and Mario emerged. At first Alex longed to return to his wife, Mario's sister, but she wouldn't think of leaving Chile. Gradually she began to consider bringing their boy. Mauricio returned to Chile at Christmas and planned to bring his bride back in March, but she wanted to keep teaching. Mario's love would leave the base at Patagonia to travel to his hemisphere. She seemed an adventurer, a daughter of the navy, and Mario started English class. He learned fast, leaning on Carlos, and he would become a great lieutenant. I helped him complete the 245i form and begin the process to legalize and make his status here permanent. Carlos worried, as the men became more skilled, they would leave him, just as he trained them enough to build his business bigger—a classic small business problem I knew only too well from my years catering.

I fed them, hoping to hold them until work on the house was finished, and handling food, trying to remember my identity: I could use my language of food with some humans willing to hear me. I made lunch, they broke bread, and they planned next tasks, discussed their family needs. They warmed up from the deep chill of working all day, outdoors. Gradually we had eye contact, then smiles, with greater ease. I talked with them just a bit, explained what I could learn about PIN numbers and immigration laws, where to buy Christmas gifts for family in Chile and other questions Carlos translated for them or Mario attempted to express.

I welcomed them to America. My grandmother, Chika, had helped *lantzmen* and family members arrive in America a hundred years ago. She generously added herring to the pot of potatoes she boiled for her boarders on Sundays, those who shared beds and rooms all week, all shifts. I could do no less. I cooked "American" for these immigrants. As they rebuilt our house, I hoped to help them build their own. The statistics, displayed graphically at Ellis Island, document the shift from East European refugees to the peoples of Latin America and Asia. I know the reality in my kitchen, over coffee, served with *empanadas* and homemade *rugelach*.

As they continued their work, I thought about the irony of our roles. Why did I mix and match menus like that? Despite their number, and the demolition surrounding me while I was home alone, I never felt vulnerable with them. I knew it was their own poverty that had first driven them to this country, where they could work because of my affluence. I wanted to share what I could with them, and I wanted them to feel kindness from one person in this country—if only in how I cooked potatoes. I was grateful for their hard work.

Curried Mushrooms on Toast

NEVER GUESSED I WOULD BE MAKING curried mushrooms on toast for lunch today. I was softening Rancho Gordo canary beans as the fresh-dripped morning coffee seeped into my veins. I thought I was going for beans and chicken broth; I'd boiled off the bones of the chicken carcass last night. I needed more to drink after my coffee infusion, and yes, I went back to my computer screen while the beans were simmering, and yes, I forgot the tea kettle again. I opened the fridge mid-morning, seeking comfort after I'd scorched the poor kettle; this one doesn't have a whistle, although all my other appliances have whistles or beeps or rings or voices telling me I've forgotten to move the laundry, turn off the dish washer, left the fridge door open. None of the appliances trust my memory.

Falling out of the fridge, because they were wedged in badly around my dear husband's collection of chocolate milk in half gallons, liters of kefir, juices, and Perrier, were the mushroom caps. I had not gotten to stuff them when his family arrived for

Passover weekend. Somehow I had brushed them clean, popped off their stems all set to stuff, but the twenty or so relatives had distracted me. They ate the eggplant caponata, pickled salmon, matzoh balls and soup, chicken breasts stuffed with porcini and dried tart cherries, roasted root vegetables, brisket with shallots and carrots, turkey rolled around spinach soufflé, vegetable frittata, a few salads (I forget what I put in those bowls), chocolate-covered matzoh toffee candy, two kinds of meringues, chocolate covered (and some plain for nephew Eli) macaroons, almond torte, caramel sauce, and fruit; they ate everything I made and served—but somehow I'd missed the mushroom caps during three days of company, so they sat downstairs in the extra fridge, waiting for me to pay them some proper attention.

It had been a few weeks, but they were still in good shape, just starting to darken and grow "funky." Leslie talked me into enjoying them like that some years ago, when I was ready to give some nasty-looking shrooms a toss. Leslie Revsin was the first woman chef at the Waldorf Astoria. She had built her reputation on her fine fish cooking. But then, she adored the smell of skunks, too. She didn't like the flavorless white button mushrooms so quickly unloaded by wholesale purveyors, so she bought her shrooms a week or two before she intended them for a menu. As they dried out, grew dark and really fungi, she appreciated their stronger, "more interesting" flavor profile. She could spin something unexpected into a recipe, and lift flavor out of some totally tasteless foodstuffs, every time. I watched her taste something and invariably *know* what was needed to make it delicious.

I learned about her flavor preferences one week when she cooked with me for a big and important catering gig. A famous restaurateur was attending a house party in Scarsdale, and I asked Leslie to help me poach the salmon. I wound up washing every pot and pan, strainer, and utensil in the house that day, as she used each one, briefly, and passed everything into the sink. The salmon was terrific. I pulled the rest of the menu and service together for that event, and I earned the chance to run a small business venture Mr. Restaurateur was backing.

Too bad the partners were lying thieves. They based their numbers of tenants on how many there would be if and when the building was totally rented. They hoped to attract those tenants based on the lovely coffee cart in the lobby, but they neglected to tell me the real numbers to base the business on. I learned I could not make money on a coffee cart business in an office building that was basically empty. I was in and out of there in two months, leaving the cart behind before the debts swallowed me. That's when my niece asked for a cousin, and I told her, "Nope, you get a coffee cart." She was a rather puzzled child for a while, but soon enough she did have her cousin, and the coffee cart was history.

When the mushrooms assaulted me this morning, I understood their imperative that I do something with them. I reached for the dill butter lying on the top shelf, then the thyme, which was edging moldy in the veggie bin. I found caramelized onions, left over from someone's omelet last weekend, and that peeled garlic (a cheat from Whole Foods) in time to use it up. It all went into the flat-bottomed Calphalon stew pot. I cranked up the heat. . .well, make-believe heat, from a home-based electric hot-top (probably why the tea kettle is still okay to use even after I've cooked it dry so many times). I hit the steaming mush-rooms with a bit of curry paste, some half-and-half (we are long on *that* today, I see), and lots of Aleppo pepper. When the mushrooms were fragrant, I toasted up the last slim slices of crusty Sullivan Street bread and ate my lunch, watching the tur-keys watching me as they waited for some crumbs to fall out the window for them to share.

Curried Mushrooms on Toast

2 pounds mushrooms, caps, slices, pieces, whatever
2 tablespoons butter
3-6 cloves of garlic, sliced (to taste)
½ large onion, or 1-2 smaller ones, diced whatever size you
   like
1 teaspoon dill, chopped
1 teaspoon thyme
¼ teaspoon pepper—Aleppo, or fresh grated if you prefer
1 teaspoon salt
¼ cup cream or half-and-half
1 teaspoon curry paste (make this with 1/2 teaspoon curry
   powder and 2 teaspoons vinegar, more powder if you
   like stronger curry taste)

Melt the butter on high heat, and add onions and garlic. When they start to take on color, add the mushrooms, then the herbs. Turn down the heat to a simmer as the mushrooms give off their liquid. Add the cream and curry paste, and reduce the liquid to thicken into a sauce for your toasts.

Toast bread slices, spoon mushrooms generously on top, and enjoy!

AT 2 O'CLOCK I GOT BACK to the canary beans. They had soaked up the basil vinaigrette I had given them to drink while the mushrooms were simmering this morning, and the dried cranberries made a nice contrast: golden beans and dark red berries, starchy/herbal softness against the chewy sweetness. They are okay with my green tea for a snack.

I KNOW IT ISN'T DINNER TIME YET, just 5:30, but that's time for cocktails somewhere. I could have nibbled something naughty (like that caramel sauce hiding on the top shelf, back left corner), but I was virtuous and nibbled some roast chicken, just to taste it with the beans. On another shelf of the fridge I found some of last night's bourbon mustard-glazed salmon, which I like cold with arugula. A few bites of that dark, sharp green makes me feel "healthy," cuts the unctuous omega oils, and titillates my eyeballs—and I enjoy the color contrast, too. I found a few dark chocolate-covered raisins in the pantry closet. They counted as dessert after the beans and the salmon course. I'm not a purist: I start some mornings with dessert, others with sautéed garlic and onion, but for now I'll just take another bite of this torte with lemon curd while I wait for Les to come home for his dinner at 9:00 p.m.

END NOTES

Thap was then. Today, catering is different, and so is my life. A sour mood emerged in the 1990s: An increased competitive edge spiked the food industry. Specialty stores expanded; more carried the luxury items that had only been available in rare shops a decade earlier. Every corner market offered a "salad bar" and more prepared foods; "home meal replacements" were available in every grocery market. Appetites and expectations changed rapidly as American palates took on significantly broader and more sophisticated world tastes, fueled in part by the fifteen hundred or more culinary schools opened around the country, significant marketing efforts by specialty food associations, and many professional organizations, including the International Association of Culinary Professionals (IACP, grown from the Association of Cooking School Teachers, into a broad-based association of food professionals, bonding those who work beyond the restaurant kitchens), Les Dames d'Escoffier, Women Chefs and Restaurateurs, Women's Food

Service Forum, and the New York Women's Culinary Alliance.

Although women attend the schools and participate, even lead many of the professional associations, I contend they are still not recognized for their true contributions to food work. Undercounted and devalued, women do not have equality, parity, sufficient voice on issues, financing for enough of their business concepts, or adequate consideration for their significantly greater family responsibilities. This is a systemic problem yet to be resolved throughout our society; I am sorry not to see greater change in the fascinating catering industry.

By the 1990s, everyone could be a caterer: Prepared foods slipped onto platters got people through events on ever-tighter budgets. I found myself bidding against individuals "catering" one or two events without paying staff, purchasing equipment, or covering the insurance and taxes I shouldered as a legit business. I worked from a second apartment with a professional lease and my landlord's approval; I paid attention to my contracts and paid state sales taxes on time.

Catering, associated with the fashion industry expansion since the 1960s, grew into higher-fashion, even greater-prestige, events. Catering was less and less about eating, breaking bread together, sharing events, and celebrating, and more about the architecture of the tray, the competitive elegance of the event, and higher pricing. From my perspective, events moved further from the importance of shared food and toward the competition championed by the TV *Food Network*. People asked me if they could contribute their own prep and planning to family parties, and fund-raising events no longer led to more lucrative private events. The not-for-profit organizations I loved to help began to offer budgets that squeezed me below my costs.

For me, catering was both intimate service and public theatre. It was *not* work you phoned in remotely; there was never a typical day at an office. To be really good was to be invisible. The host/hostess was the star. For my catering service, I pulled open the curtain and directed timing and movement of all the players, but my service was best when I was not seen, only felt, as a secure, steady force, totally in charge and making an event happen "right." I directed a food-based performance art. Those gifted as performers did well in service for catering companies: Other skills were needed offstage in the kitchen, and the best team members, the kindest, became "family" in our traveling company. We were our own party; the joyful kitchen crew, the entertainment and timing of dancers, actors, and singers reading physical cues, and their improvised choreography made or ruined an event, "the show," without client's conscious awareness. The foods, the buffet sets, were the focus—not the cooks, or me as a business owner. Disasters and near-disasters revealed who had the skills, the calm demeanor and self-control to "perform" catering. So much was beyond the food: in the organization, the details of the "set," the correct staffing and timing. I was not paying ten dollars an hour (still the current rate at some large-scale operations, with the expectation that a gratuity might make the work more lucrative; staff are now paid closer to fifteen dollars an hour in New York, as minimum wage). In the 1980s, I was paying ten to twenty-five dollars an hour for quality staff, not minimum quality. When I was small,

I could practice my own personnel policies; I could split a prep shift between a grandma and a new mom. I could give away food to a hungry staff member or grant time off for auditions, which I encouraged.

Catering was fascinating work for me for many years: It was artistic, creative teamwork, public performance art, and intimate connection all at the same time. What happened in the kitchen, and what happened on the floor, could be two simultaneous dramas, totally different but parallel scripts. What could be more intimate than eating food prepared by someone in your own kitchen? What could be more public than a fund-raising event in a national historic landmark? Catering work was smart, witty, delicious, and caring. It was so much more than the ingredients, the recipes, or the dishes lined up on a buffet for profit.

Over the years, I watched many women, seduced by the love of food and images of nurturing, march into the belly of the food industry beast to work in hideous, dysfunctional kitchens, never seeing a customer's satisfaction, never sharing in the affective connections that first drew them into the culinary world. The struggle was always to stay close to the food, find ways to grow, and develop skills and knowledge without losing touch with personal goals and individual life. The compromises and transitions were harsh, demanding, and limiting, especially for women seeking to create family lives, which had to be carefully planned and closely monitored; and *still* I saw too many relationships fail.

Other goals, interests, and obligations began to distract me from matching the feathered garnishes on canapés lined up for service to Park Avenue guests who could not care less. Mistakes could mean the end of my business: a lawsuit, someone made sick by mishandled food, something broken by a careless turn. I am proud none of these things occurred in fifteen years, but I began to fear it was only a matter of time, of circumstance.

When my business was small I could believe I was running it as I saw fit, whether that ideal was true or my illusion: My feeling was of freedom and control over my life and choices. As it grew, the business began to consume my life. I was on call at all times, for all emotions, to work under any conditions. I felt that, if I said "no," I would not grow—until I reached the point when, finally, as the twentieth century drew to a close, I lacked the drive to make my small service into a large company. I was not willing to invest in major growth, to shift my client base, to compete with the "big dogs." I could not afford to work as I had, close to staff and clients. Those deeper meanings of food, the relationships among food workers, and with clients, were cut away from catering as a business. I had lost a great deal of heart, the requisite driving energy, and perhaps some courage over the years; I had lost Michael, and catering was no longer the challenging, amusing work it had been for me. Was that the end of my "success"?

Moving from managing a business to the business running my life was not a happy spot. It took fancy footwork for years to keep my balance, and yet only my own business choices or my own hearth made me feel "successful." I didn't want to be ground down, exhausted by work on someone else's hot cooking line. I often assured myself, "I can always cook for a living," but as I aged, I was not eager to join that line. I believed I could always "freelance" catering, to catch some money here and there, but today, I still see no really steady place close to the food for a woman over fifty, if it isn't her own hearth or her own business.

So it came time to change over to other options and reset my priorities, to teach, to write, to work in food styling, to judge baking contests and cookbook awards, to escort food authors, and then to complete my doctorate, take care of my parents and family, a house, and my own health. . .and the rest of my life, now that food is hot.

Kevan Full

ABOUT THE AUTHOR

Carol G. Durst-Wertheim, Ph.D., has taught culinary arts, food studies, internships in the culinary arts, catering, dietary management, hospitality research, food geography, and culinary tourism at New York Metropolitan universities.

The first Director of the New York Restaurant School at the New School for Social Research, she owned New American Catering Corporation, wrote *I Knew You Were Coming So I Baked a Cake* (Simon & Schuster, 1997), and completed an oral history for the New York Women's Culinary Alliance.

Her writing appears in encyclopedia and essay collections. She leads film discussions for adults and has served on the Boards of the Women Chefs and Restaurateurs, Infinite Family, and the Federated Conservationists of Westchester County.

She has been paid for more than two dozen legitimate kinds of food work, most not counted by the U.S. Department of Labor, hence "invisible." She continues to seek ways to bring the food conversation to broader audiences.

CPSIA information can be obtained
at www.ICGtesting.com
Printed in the USA
LVHW030551130720
660468LV00003B/223

9 781946 989505